Unmasking The Book of Revelation

by
Charles W. Weller

Copyright 1996
by
Charles W. Weller

ISBN 0-9653851-0-8

Published by
Not I But Christ
P.O. Box 532
Hilliard, Ohio, 43026

Printed by
Florida Theological Seminary, Inc.
126 East Colonial Drive
Orlando, Florida, 32801

For other publication, or to schedule Seminars
with Dr. Charles W. Weller contact:
Not I But Christ
P.O. Box 532
Hilliard, Ohio, 43026

Dedicated to Joyce who has helped throughout our ministry, my children for inspiring me and assisting me in Christ, to the brethren at large but in particular to Brother Bill Britton and B.S. Westlake who were my mentors.

Table of Contents

Heading	Pages
Chapter 1: Two Schools of Theology: Historical and Futuristic	5-14
Chapter 2: The Parousia	15-23
Chapter 3: The Apocalypse	24-31
Chapter 4: The Revelation of the Temple	32-60
Chapter 5: Angels	61-68
Chapter 6: Seraphim	69-73
Chapter 7: Cherubim	74-86
Chapter 8: The Beastly Image	87-94
Chapter 9: The Apostasy	95-116
Chapter 10: The Image of Christ - Sons of God	117-133
Chapter 11: Firstfruits/Oneness	134-146
Chapter 12: Lamb or Lambkin	147-152
Chapter 13: One Like Unto	153-158
Summary	159-160

FORWARD

The written word is judged over time whether it is worthy of serious consideration. Some religious books express doctrine which over time can be proven to be erroneous. Other religious books are written for a certain time and the issues of that era.

Ours is not purported to be a definitive work. Neither is it a doctrinal work, although some might try to classify it as such. This small volume is a compilation of thoughts of this author who over a period of time grasped certain spiritual principles that led to a different viewpoint or interpretation of the book of Revelation.

In times past volumes have been written about the historical and literal fulfillment of the book of Revelation. This line of thought was quite prevalent before 1800 AD. Martin Luther tied the antichrist into the Pope of the Roman church. Others also wrote and expressed their interpretations. It is not ours to discuss the historical fulfillment of the book of Revelation, but we would suggest that there seems to be great truth in such a line of thought.

I believe there is a weakness with the historical viewpoint. By developing an historical approach to interpretation, the book of Revelation becomes antiquated and not of current interest to the Christian faith. If it has been fulfilled then what is written in the volume is not helpful to our Christian walk today. I think scripture is timeless with its relevancy for our faith.

Then there is the futuristic school of interpretation of the book of Revelation. This view became more prominent in the 1800's and is the rule of the current day - 1995. From this futuristic school come some of the following religious beliefs: rapture, second coming, literal lake of fire, literal hell with many levels, etc. But if study is carefully done, one will see that Lacunza, a Jesuit priest, fostered the idea of the rapture, and others created additional material to relieve the pressure on the Roman church by Christians (Luther, Calvin, etc.) who understood that the Roman church had accepted many pagan beliefs which were contrary to the holy scriptures.

By developing a futuristic philosophy the book of Revelation has no current value to a person of the Christian faith and relieves the person from "today's" responsibility in many ways concerning his faith. By making the beast some unknown monster, when in reality it is the carnal nature that is at enmity with God, or by misidentifying the harlot from the religious system whether Protestant, Catholic or Moslem etc., the futuristic school of interpretation places all events in the future and denigrates the book of Revelation into many false interpretations. In my lifetime alone I have heard that the mark of the beast was the social security card, that all of the following were the antichrist: Hitler, Kissinger, Gorbachev (especially some preached because of the mark on his forehead). None of these were correct nor could be.

Thus, it is the concern of this author to offer another interpretation to the Book of Revelation. I believe that the book of Revelation is not the revealing of the beast, nor the harlot, nor the lake of fire, etc. Neither is it a certain mark on the hand or the forehead in a literal stamp of some sort or perhaps a computer chip as some see it now.

I believe that there is a certain spiritual principle that governs all interpretations of the Bible that must be the very foundation of each person's faith. This principle is so fundamental that many do not perceive the depth nor the height of it let alone its breadth. <u>Any theology that externalizes your faith, that is to say any religious thought</u>

<u>that proclaims as truth some thing that is not dealing with you in your personal development of a marriage relationship with Jesus Christ is erroneous</u>.

Truth is not a fact, neither is it knowledge. Truth is a person, Christ Jesus our Lord. There is not another name whereby a man can be saved, and such a nature is above every name. <u>Any theology (God study) that directs your attention to outward signs on the earth or in the sky is a religious deception, even though it might have knowledge in it</u>. For while it gives you knowledge, we know that knowledge puffs up but love edifies (1 Corinthians 8:1).

Each book of the Bible is a revelation of Him who is the Book of Life in which we are written, living epistles written to be read of all men. Therefore the Book of Revelation is a revelation of Him (1:1). I see the book as the manifestation of Christ Jesus in a person. As He sits down within the vessel taking His throne, He dispossesses the beast and the harlot nature etc. Then we see the glorious victory of the cross manifested in the saint.

I would not be so foolish as to state that I have complete understanding of this book - I think it would be a lifetime work that would never be accomplished. But what I feel is truth (truth is not a "what" but a greater revelation of "Who"), I will share. Hopefully, the reader will be gracious and allow some latitude.

The world cries out for the coming of the Lord. The Hebrews missed the manifestation of the Lord because He did not fit their religious concept based upon their own understanding of the scriptures. The current church system also looks for the coming of the Lord. I fear they too are looking erroneously for a literal man, coming to set up a literal kingdom, even as the Hebrews did. The truth that resides in the book of Revelation is the fulfilling of Romans

8:19-21 and Galatians 2:20. These two verses are the basis of our interpretation of the book of Revelation

It is the outworking of our inner nature (Him) that we behold as we look at the book of Revelation. Before we enter into the discussion of the book itself, it is important to lay a foundation so that the reader might at least follow and understand what we write.

If there is disagreement with what we write, place this volume's thoughts on a shelf. But do not discard. For if what we write is spiritual life, your Lord and Savior will bring it to remembrance causing it to quicken your mortal mind.

May what we write bring glory to Him and edify the Lord's body.

Chapter One

TWO SCHOOLS of THEOLOGY:
Historical and Futuristic

The one school believes that most of the Bible has been completed. The other believes that most of the Bible is yet future. The Reformation, which was a movement to change what we today call the Roman Catholic church, was begun in the 800's by the Waldenese. It culminated with Martin Luther's 96 points of suggested change on a Wittenberg Abbey door in Germany in 1517. He was followed very shortly by other men of great caliber such as Knox and Calvin, not to mention the advent of the printing press by Gutenberg who expedited the explosion of knowledge through the printed page, something which never happened before.

Luther, in his writings, calls the Pope the antichrist and clearly shows why in Scriptures. As one studies the writings of Luther he explains his historical interpretation. If one wants to study secular history you will find that some Popes were women and had children. At one time there were two Popes fighting for supremacy, one in France and one in Rome. If one wishes to study, we suggest the book, **Two Babylons -Papal Worship** by Alexander Hislop, 1959 or **Babylon - Mystery Religion** by Ralph Woodrow. These two books give a detailed history of why the Protestant leaders were so against the corrupt church system.

It would shock many evangelical Christians to learn that their theology comes from the Roman Catholic church. A Jesuit, named Ribera (1537-1591) who first taught that Daniel and Revelation were "futuristic" in their fulfillment, began a line of theological thinking that would be expanded upon. The Roman church was losing thousands of people a day from their church as the people heard and agreed with the Reformers. The bleeding Roman Church was trying to staunch the flow of income it was losing and also was trying to take the "heat" off of itself by showing through a new theology that it was not the antichrist but rather it was yet to come. Another priest, Cardinal Bellarmine, helped Ribera in his charade.

The historical school of theology shows how the book of Revelation is and was completed many years ago. The futuristic school of theology looks for a physical antichrist, one man, a seven or at least a three and one-half year tribulation and a millennial reign of Christ. These concepts all came out of the works of Jesuits who wrote to confound and redirect Protestant ire. We are not going to write on those subjects but it is interesting to note that John states that the antichrist was already there in the first century!

Two books which explain why there is no seven year or even three and one-half year tribulation are **What the Bible Says About the Great Tribulation** by William Kimball and **The Parousia** by Stuart Russell. John Bray has written a pamphlet showing why the pre-tribulation rapture is wrong entitled **The Origin of the Pre-Tribulation Rapture Teaching**. These men refer to Ribera and a Jesuit priest, Lacunza, who did substantial writing in the 1800's to foster the development of a futuristic theology.

The Lutheran Theological Seminary in Philadelphia has a book entitled **The Coming Messiah** written by Rabbi Ben Ezra which was the pen name of Emamual Lacunza. This book had a major impact on the Protestant move. The

Protestants believed that from the Dark Ages (4th century) to the Reformation was the reign of the antichrist. The Roman church held the idea that from 1580-1830 the antichrist was a person yet to come.

Unfortunately, present day Protestants (anyone that is not a Roman Catholic) have preached such silly things as Mussolini as the antichrist, then Hitler, then Kissinger, then Gorbachev (some even said he had the mark on his forehead!). Some thought and preached the social security system was the mark of the beast in the 1930's. Then we have heard the evangelicals state that the ten toes of the man in Daniel is represented by the common market members. As of 1992 there are 13 members and more applying. So goes carnal theology.

The teaching of the futuristic theology entered evangelical Christianity in the 1800's. Lacunza wrote his book showing that Jesus must return twice not once as Scripture states. This secret coming was a rapture. This way the saints could escape the coming "tribulation" and the "antichrist". The Archbishop of Canterbury in England read the book and the idea became prevalent in the Anglican church (USA counterpart Episcopal).

Secondly, Bill Britton brings out in his pamphlet **The Rapture of the Church 'what is it'?** that Edward Irving, who was the founder of the Catholic Apostolic Church, preached the idea of a rapture. This man was a Scottish Presbyterian minister who had accepted the idea of Lacunza and then was filled with the "baptism of the Spirit" and left the church to formulate a Pentecostal church. He, unfortunately, brought with him some of the theology of the Roman church. His church was in London. During a service there a young woman named Margaret McDonald spoke in prophecy concerning a secret rapture.

Another source was J. N. Darby, a Christian man who was considered perhaps as the founder of the Brethren Movement. He was an Anglican and attended meetings in Ireland concerning the secret rapture. Some sources indicate that he was involved with McDonald in some way. Scofield incorporated in his Bible the notes of Darby on various verses, without consideration of his thoughts. Scofield's Bible became very popular since many people could read it and study his footnotes. People read the Bible and footnotes and were greatly influenced in their teaching by the notes -as they are today.

These three men - Lacunza, Irving, Darby - are responsible for the premise of a rapture. But if one has such an idea then other factors have to come into play. The tribulation, what about it? John 17:15 truly answers that - *"I pray not that you* (disciples) *should be taken out of the world, but that you* (Father) *should keep them from evil."* Or consider Matthew 5 which states: "the meek shall inherit the earth", or even the Lord's Prayer which states in Matthew 6 *"Your kingdom come and your will be done <u>on earth</u> as it is in heaven."* There are many more verses that show the saints remain, even if there is a tribulation.

The Bible Verses Millennial Teachings by George C. Lubbers on page 237 states the following: " We desire the reader to keep in mind that we are not interested in giving a history of Dr. Scofield's work, dating about 1843 (which incidentally was a time when such heresies as Christian Science, Mormonism and Seventh Day Adventism appeared) but we are interested in some of the basic teachings and constructions, which are today the structural teaching of Dispensationalism in America." There are two points here. First, the point that Scofield's ideas of futuristic thought were new with dispensational ideas (dispensational meaning the Bible is divided up into certain time elements as to eschatology [study of final things]). Secondly, there was much paganism that had been created with a "Christian flavor" - Mormonism, Christian Science and now also Scofield's ideas which had come from Lacunza.

It is important to note that each of these other movements created or were looking for some future kingdom to come. Mormonism looked for the kingdom to come. The Reorganized Latter Day Saints church and Mormons have purchased a lot of land around the Kansas City, Missouri, area for the expectation that the kingdom will be set up there. The Seventh Day Adventists were noted in 1844 for going to the mountains and selling all they had for the literal return of Jesus. Unfortunately, the same thing happened in Korea in 1988 and it was false, as was the book that was printed in the USA proclaiming such. Christian Science taught that this life was unreal and that if you were active in your mind, you could deny sickness saying that it didn't exist. Quite metaphysical. While it is true that some sickness is psychosomatic or mind-induced, you cannot deny its effect.

Lubbers goes on to expose the error of dispensationalism as Scofield presents it. Scofield said there was no grace until Christ. But Noah found, as the scripture declares, "grace" in the eyes of the Lord. Scofield limits 'the Promise' to the chronological time between Abraham and Mount Sinai, the time of the 'Law giving', he has made it impossible for himself (Scofield) to do justice to the great 'Promise' as given already by God Himself in Paradise to Adam and Eve at the very dawn of History."(pg. 244).

Rev. Lubbers was of the Reformed Church and preached over 50 years in the USA. His research is highly regarded and expresses the thought of the Reformers rather than the Jesuit's teachings. There are many that will and can expose Dr. Scofield's notes for their errors. Again most of his notes came from his relationship with Darby and the Irving Movement.

The futuristic school of theology propounds the theology which includes the following: a return of Christ personally, a secret rapture (either before the tribulation, in mid-tribulation or after the tribulation), a tribulation of seven or a time period of two three and one half years, an antichrist who will rule until overthrown, a literal millennial (meaning 1,000 year) reign of Christ, followed by the release of Satan to rule the world and delude it again and the end of time with people either in the New Jerusalem, seen as a literal place, and the wicked outside the city burning in the lake of fire. While there may be some variation along these lines of thought, these come from the major theology of the Lacunza and Tractarian societies and the Roman Church.

The historical theological viewpoint is that the book of Revelation is spiritual and not literal since the actual literal fulfillment has already occurred. Secondly, the historical generally expresses the point that the numbers found in the book of Revelation and other places are allegorical or symbolical and are not for literal interpretation. The futuristic school would contend this otherwise. The Weston Bible has footnotes which support the historical point of view and the Scofield Bible has notes which propose the futuristic point of view.

A Third View of Theology

Then there is the third school that is neither historical nor futuristic but believes that the historical probably did occur and that the futuristic probably will not occur. The reason for such an idea is that these people look for a spiritual fulfillment within people. They look to find Christ fully formed in the individual. Secondly these people believe that the antichrist, the man of sin, and the false prophet are found within each person because of the fallen nature and that each must be removed. The antichrist spirit is the spirit of a man. The false prophet is the soul of a man. The man of sin is the actions of the body.

One of these schools is correct. Generally in the evangelical churches today there is a preponderance of the futuristic school and little credence is given to the historical school. Even less credence is given to the belief that both the man of sin and Christ can dwell in a person. Many saints are not aware that there are other views. The saints believe what is taught without any question. Most saints are not Bereans who study to show themselves approved daily (Acts 17, 2 Timothy 2:15).

I believe that to properly interpret the book of Revelation a person must understand that the coming of Christ has to be internal. His manifestation in us begins with our salvation (feast of Passover) experience, continues with his infilling of the Spirit (John 20:22) and empowerment (Acts 2 - feast of Pentecost) and is completed in full union with Him (feast of Tabernacles).

The whole foundation of the New Testament is the premise that Jesus Christ came to enter into a personal relationship with each individual. He died on the cross and resurrected in order to free us from the bondage of sin and corruption so that we might enter boldly to the throne of grace and have fellowship with the Father. This fellowship was to be personal, intimate and fulfilling and above all spiritual. To discuss this concept further we must understand the comings of the Lord and what they mean, especially as to how they relate to the book of Revelation.

As an example in Revelation 1:10 it states that John was caught up on the Lord's Day. Yet, all of the saints in the faith look with anticipation for the "coming day of the Lord." The Church based in futuristic theology tradition has taught us over the last 150 years that the man Jesus is going to return at some future time. Yet, John declares that he was caught up on the Lord's day. There would seem to be a serious theological problem here. Is the day to come or has it already come?

Yet, we must be aware that there is a problem only if we are dealing with chronological time. For this type of time creates a time line that extends horizontally. The word "kronos" is Greek in its origin and in the English corresponds with "clock or watch" time concept. Based upon this definition of time, all saints after John have missed the coming of the Lord. While Paul says the Lord has not come yet in Thessalonians, that book was written well before John's book of Revelation as John was the last to die.

As a side note, we find that John states that there were many antichrists already working in his day (1 John 2:18, 2 John 1:7). Perhaps, this has also caused consternation with others as to how the antichrist was to come and yet was already there. There must be an interpretation that is correct which will make 1 John and Revelation compatible rather than divergent. Fortunately, God's word does not disagree with itself because it is a unit, one in purpose from Genesis through Revelation. In fact, every seemingly disagreeable point can be explained so that there is no disagreement.

What then is the solution to the "Lord's Day" coming in the book of Revelation to John? Why then have we missed it? Well, we have not. The Lord's Day has nothing to do with chronological time but is directly related to "kairos" time. This is another Greek word that speaks of time in the sense of relationship. The Lord's Day began in you when He came into your life. The growth of His Day has no end in you for each day is a time of enlarging. Just as a child does not sense that it is growing and changing on a daily basis, neither do you sense the spiritual growth in you. Spiritual growth is "relationship" time.

John was caught up on the Lord's Day. He first was already in the Spirit and had a spiritual relationship with the Father. In order to be "caught up", he had to be in a spiritual place walking with God so that he could respond to "come up hither." In order for a complete release for creation from the bondage of corruption, it first must begin with "kairos" time. If there is not a depth of relationship with God, then there will not be the manifestation of the life of God in the sons of God (Romans 8:19-20) to release creation at a chronological point.

The truth is that the fulfillment of God's eternal plan on the natural plane has to occur simultaneously with "kairos" and "kronos" time. The one, "kairos", is the vertical shaft of the cross. It speaks of God and Man's relationship with each other. The other, "kronos", is the horizontal shaft of the cross and it speaks of the time line in the natural sequence. If either of these is not in the right position at the right time, the moment passes.

Relationship time removes one out of the temporal and places one in eternity. As one begins to move into Him, natural things begin to look different. J.T. Fraser in his book, **The Voices of Time**, states: "A person's view of time is a method of discerning his personality". Society in the USA and Western culture in particular is always planning for the future. This affects our religious outlook because we as a people look for eschatological events (end time things).

But have you gone to Africa? Here is a different culture. The saints there that I have met are not concerned with the future coming of the Lord. It is rarely discussed (unless with a Western missionary) because they are concerned with the "now" or relational time. We must value internal time which values the "event" and not the duration of it. "Jet lag" is the result of our internal clock being out of place with the chronological clock. William McConnell states: "If time is a love gift, something to be shared - to be invested, but invested with people - could it be that we are missing something when we relate our time solely to efficiency and accomplishment?"

To consider time as a resource with a finite end, for it to "run out" is not a true perception. The concept of "redeeming time" has come to mean "gain extra time." When in reality "redeeming time" means to create relationships and those things of eternal value. "Redeeming time" means to make the most of every opportunity for the advancement of the kingdom of God by revealing your nature found in Christ. "Be instant in season and out of season" is a message of Timothy. When one is in this relationship, "kairos" time, one flows with life. But if one is in "kronos" time, this does not occur.

The Lord's Day is not necessarily some chronological event that will occur, but in the reality of John is an internal, spiritual event which should cause a change, a chronological event. Ponder the Lord's Day as an internal working and revealing as we progress through the book of Revelation.

Chapter 2

THE COMING OF THE LORD - "PAROUSIA"

There are many words for the "coming" of the Lord. The first that we shall deal with is that of **"parousia."** In the King James and other translations it is generally seen in English as "coming." Nowhere in the New Testament does this word relate at all to a physical "coming" of the Lord. In fact, if one studies the scriptures carefully, the phrase "second coming" is not found in the Bible. As a side note, "rapture" is not mentioned either. Both statements that have been taught as truth, come based on an erroneous interpretation of the scriptures.

The Greek word **"parousia"** means **"presence"** of the Lord. Wherever two or three are gathered together, He is there. That is, His presence is there. That is a coming.

John 14:12 states that Jesus must go "back to the Father." Who was Jesus' Father? John 4:21 reveals that God is a Spirit. God does not have flesh and bone. This is indicated in Matthew 16:17 and Luke 24:39 as Jesus compares Himself to God. 1 Timothy 1:17 states: ***"Now, unto the King eternal, immortal, invisible....."*** This also tells us that God is invisible to the human eye.

Now, then if Jesus left (He was the first coming), how does He appear to us and is it just one more time or many appearances? Again as we look at John 14:17-18 Jesus states that if He leaves, the Spirit of Truth will come to the disciples. He goes on further to state that the Comforter (that Spirit of Truth) which is Himself as a Spirit will come to them (vs. 18).

When did Jesus come? At Pentecost. The Greek word for spirit is "pneuma." It is the same word that is used in the book of Acts as "wind." Jesus came and empowered the disciples. But He did more than that. Just as salvation (the feast of Passover, 1 Corinthians 5:8) is experiential, so also is Pentecost. These men had placed within their own vessel the "presence" or the "coming" of the Lord.

Clearly, 1 Corinthians 15:45 states that Jesus (last Adam) was made a "quickening Spirit." The word "quickening" means to vivify, to make that which is dead alive. So, when these men received the Holy Spirit on the day of Pentecost, they were "quickened" or "made alive" by the Spirit which possessed them. In other words the power of the resurrection, that resurrection life, which is spiritual life (Greek "zoe", not the Greek "bios" which means natural life) had come within them to abide.

This too is a fulfillment of John 14:21-23. where Jesus states that when He returns to the Father that the two of them shall make their abode in the person. Thus, heaven is not a literal place in the sense of religious tradition which indicates that heaven is the "sky," but rather that heaven is found where God is, which is in you (Luke 17:21). *"He that is joined to the Lord is one Spirit"* (1 Cor. 6:17).

We cannot leave this thought without reviewing Ephesians 4:10 which states: *"He that descended is the same also that ascended up far above all heavens, that He might fill all things."* The coming of the Spirit at Pentecost, which is still a viable experience for all Christendom, is part of the fulfilling of Ephesians 4:10. Hopefully it is seen then that His coming, His presence, is a spiritual experience and we hope to show that the "parousia" is not a one time event but an ongoing occurrence.

So far then we have discussed, albeit briefly, a "coming" of the Lord. The problem with most saints is that they fail to comprehend, due to religious teachings of the babylonish church system, that we no longer know Christ after the flesh. When the name Jesus is said there is an immediate picture of a man about 33 years old in a robe. This is not Jesus. He has ascended and is a Spirit that has possessed His people at salvation (a coming), at Pentecost (a coming) and at Tabernacles (a coming). Paul admonishes us in 2 Corinthians 5:16: *"Though we have known Christ after the flesh, yet, now henceforth know we Him no more."*

How do we know Him then? 1 John 4:20 states that we see His coming as we see Him in another. For how can we love God whom we have not seen, if we cannot love our brother whom we have seen? Loving God is loving our neighbor, for He is in them as John 1:9 states. The question is how do we see Him - as He was or as He is?

His coming is in His saints. 1 Thessalonians 1:10 states that He will be glorified *"IN His saints."* John 14:20 states that He is IN us. That is how He is glorified - by His "coming," His "presence" in us. There is no doubt of this for Revelation 21:3 states that *"...the tabernacle of God is with men and He shall dwell* (Greek : be at home, reside in,) *with them."*

Because of traditional religious teaching which emphasizes external concepts of Christianity, many Christians have not appropriated the truth of Him who lives within. Thus, they have difficulty with delineation of the truths found in the scriptures. As an example, most saints mix up "IN His saints" and "WITH His saints" as being synonymous and both dealing with a "second" coming. Nothing could be further from the truth.

Perhaps to radically portray the coming of Christ, we should consider some verses which show a coming of Christ. 1 Thessalonians 4 reveals Christ coming as a "shout." Jude 14 He comes with His saints. 1 Thessalonians 1:10 He comes in His saints. Matthew 16:27 states He comes with angels. Have you considered His coming as the Morning Star arising in your heart (1 Peter)? In Revelation He comes as the white horse. Matthew has the Son of Man appearing as lightning . The comings of the Lord are the manifestations of His presence - whether it be the whirlwind that Elijah saw, the donkey that Baalim heard speak or the angels that visited Abraham.

I do hope that as a diligent Berean, you will search the scriptures for yourself to verify these things mentioned thus far. For there are other words also used for the coming of the Lord. The nuances are important for each reveals a greater glory of God.

A Specific Coming - 1 John 2:28

Not only Jesus but also John the Baptist called the people of Israel unto repentance. John the Baptist stated the kingdom of heaven was at hand as did Jesus (Matthew 3:2, 4:17). Jesus even told the disciples that the kingdom of God was at hand and that they should preach such as they traveled (Matthew 10:7). Jesus warned the people of a coming judgment (Matthew 11:20-24). All these verses point to a consummation soon to take place, but we know that it was not during the time of Jesus because it was "nigh" meaning close but some time off - not immediate.

Now in Matthew 12:38 - 45 we find Jesus warning "this generation." He was talking to the Hebrews of the day and not some future generation since the time of judgment was "nigh." The parable of the fig tree on the historical interpretation refers to Israel and it being cut off. Jesus even states in the parable of the tares that: "*He that soweth the good seed is the Son of Man.*" He is warning the people of the judgment to come.

In Matthew 10:23 Jesus tells His disciples when persecution comes to flee to another city, but that they shall not go over the cities until the Son of Man comes. Perhaps reading the following in conjunction will show that some of the disciples would be alive at His coming (Matthew 16:27, 28, Mark 8:38, 9:1, Luke 9:26,27). This means some of the disciples would have died before it occurs but that others would see the fulfillment of the "parousia" of the Lord.

Ultimately, the parable of the wicked husbandmen (Matthew 21:33-46, Mark 12:1-12, Luke 20:9-19) refers in the historical sense to the Hebrews who were the leaders of the nation of Israel at the time of Christ. This parable seems to relate the destruction of Israel with the coming of the Lord (Matthew 16:27-28).

In 70 AD came the fall of Jerusalem. The Romans overthrew the Hebrew religious/political leaders. The Romans destroyed the temple and removed once and for all animal sacrifice for sin, which Jesus had removed spiritually at the cross. He would return again without need for sacrifice but to establish His kingdom scripture states.

The word "world" used in Matthew 24 refers to the whole chapter in the sense of "age" or dispensation and not the same as "world" as we use it today. Matthew 24 reveals Jesus talking in prophecy of the destruction of the temple (Matthew 24:1-2) and the judgment of that particular time, the end of the age.

It cannot be reiterated enough that "parousia" means "presence", not a literal physical return of the Lord. Roman soldiers were the physical presence of the Lord that came in judgment on Israel of which some of the disciples were still alive to see.

The end of the age occurred with the judgment of Israel by the "parousia" of the Lord. Just as the Lord sent the nation of Babylon to attack Judah and to come as His "presence" in judgment on the nation of Judah and lead the people into captivity.

The coming/parousia can be personal as in 1 Corinthians 16:17 but in most cases it speaks of a spiritual fulfillment. Or the parousia can take on a spiritual sense (2 Corinthians 7:7) when an individual comes. In 2 Corinthians this refers to the consolation that came with Titus. Perhaps we should put that in contrast with the judgment that came with the Romans.

What we are trying to proclaim is that the "presence" or "parousia" of the Lord is not limited to Jesus the man nor Christ Jesus our ascended Lord. In fact, the "parousia" could, with further elucidation, probably prove that there is no need for a physical return but rather that the "presence" of Him in a people is a type of "coming" of the Lord.

Paul writes in 2 Corinthians 10:10 " 'For his letters', they say 'are weighty and powerful, but his bodily presence (Greek here, parousia) is weak..'" Here we find that the word "parousia" is used with the concept of "presence" and not really dealing with Paul's small physical stature, although a factor, but rather dealing with the "power of the presence" that Paul brought. Paul writes in 1 Thessalonians 5:23 that God *"sanctify you completely; and may your whole spirit, soul and body be preserved blameless at the "coming" of our Lord Jesus Christ."* Here again, the "presence" of the Lord is His coming to be glorified IN His saints (2 Thessalonians 1:10).

2 Thessalonians 2:1 speaks of the parousia again. Here it is in relation to the Lord's appearance in the temple (Greek - NAOS) which refers to the body as the temple (1 Corinthians 3:17). The word for physical structure in the Greek is *heiron* which means a building. So the coming of the Lord, the parousia is His appearing in the saint causing the man of sin in this chapter to be cast off - the fallen Adamic nature. For those with a historical frame of reference it could be used to tie into the "presence" of the Lord with the Roman emperor standing in the literal Hebrew temple thus defiling the physical temple BUT this cannot be true since the word here for temple refers to your physical body and not a building.

The key to understanding "parousia" is that it refers to the invisible power of God being expressed through a vessel of His choosing, whether a saint or a pagan who is doing His bidding. The "parousia" does not refer to the literal manifestation of the man Jesus nor to our ascended Lord physically returning. It can and does refer to our Lord who appears in and through us for His glory.

John writes in 1 John that we may have confidence at His appearing/ coming (1 John 2:28). Many would interpret that to be a personal return of the man Jesus. But if 1 John 4:20 is considered with this verse, as it should be since the letter is a "whole," there is a deep truth. How can we love the ascended Lord who is Spirit, if we cannot love His appearing or "presence" in a person whom we do see? The truth of the "parousia" or "coming" of the Lord is the recognition of His "presence" in His people.

But the "parousia" is just the first part of four parts of His appearing that will be made manifest through each saint. The "parousia" is just the first step on the path to the complete manifestation of who He is in us. Again we see that

Peter in 2 Peter 1:16 refers to the "coming" of the Lord to whom he was an eyewitness. How did Peter know the man Jesus was the Son of God? It was the presence of God that revealed it to him. Otherwise Jesus was not comely to look as Isaiah foretold.

Recognizing the "coming" of the Lord as the "presence" of the Lord whether in a Roman general or a saint is to say that we see the hand of God moving over the face of the deep. For the Lord moves mysteriously to fulfill His purposes on a grand scale in the tides of the affairs of men and also in the individual's life. The recognizing the "presence" of the Lord in one's life is a prerequisite before the student can begin to study the second stage of the manifestation of the Lord.

There are three other words used for the coming of the Lord which are: apocalypse, epiphany and appearing. We shall consider the apocalypse as it relates to the fulfilling of the book of Revelation. After the "presence" of Christ in you is known experientially by the believer the next step is the awareness of the apocalypse "coming" of the Lord in your life which the book of Revelation discusses.

There are many words for "coming" of the Lord. Four main ones are easily identified. It is best explained by the Hebrew-Greek Key study Bible edited by Spiros Zohhiates and printed by AMG Publishers, Chattanooga, TN. "Phaneroo means to make manifest, make known, show in the NT, synonomous with apokalupto to reveal, remove a lid. Therefore in this sense it means to denote the act of divine revelation (John 17:6, Rom.1:19, 3:21, 16:26, Colossians 1:26, 2 Timothy 1:10, Titus 1:3, Hebrews 9:8, 1 John 1:2, 4:9). It differs from apokalupto as 'to exhibit' differs from 'to disclose' so that in relation to each other apokalupto must precede phaneroo (1 Corinthians 3:13).

Apokalupto refers only to the object revealed but phaneroo refers to those to the revelation is made (cf. Ephesians 3:5, Colossians 1:26, 3:4, 4:4, Titus 1:3)."

So, there is 'parousia', 'phaneroo', 'epiphany' and 'apocalypse'. Each has its place in the plan of God to be used in the development of the saint's personal walk in Christ. We shall next consider 'apocalypse' because of its importance to the book of Revelation.

Chapter Three

THE APOCALYPSE

The first verse in the book of Revelation states: "The revelation of Jesus Christ." The Greek word for the English "revelation" is "apocalypse." This word is distinctly different from "presence." It is first used by Simeon at Jesus' dedication found in Luke 2:32. The translation would read: "A light 'unveiled' to the Gentiles and the glory of Your people Israel." For the word "apocalypse" means the "unveiling" predominately.

Simeon was proclaiming that the Savior was now <u>manifested</u>, <u>made visible</u>, <u>distinguished from all others</u>, a <u>complete revelation</u> of the invisible God made visible to the world. Simeon's prophecy proclaimed the completed manifestation of the Lord. What do we mean the completed manifestation, revelation? Just this, the fulfilling of 1 Corinthians 15:28. For the true "unveiling" of Christ Jesus is that in the fullness of time His victory on the cross over death will gather together all things whether in the earth, under the earth or above the earth (Ephesians 1:10, Philippians 2:10, Colossians 1:16-17).

The Gospels reveal a progressive revelation of Jesus Christ. The letters of the New Testament reveal the glorious ascended Lord who has descended into His people. Luke reveals the "man" side of Jesus where he states: *"And Jesus increased in wisdom and stature and in favor with God and man"* (Luke 2:52). The Lord's path, planned from its inception, was designed to reveal to the world the fullness of God could be manifested in a man.

As the life of Jesus is our pattern to follow (1 Peter 2:21, Philippians 3:17), <u>we find that what He did was to learn who He was until the time of His manifestation</u> at the Jordan River. Every step of His life from birth until His appearance in ministry after being in the wilderness was designed by the Father to teach Him who He was.

It is important to note while the dedication revealed who Jesus was, it did not change the blindness of the people to who He was! For even though He was manifested then, He was not received but by a very few and those only knew by revelation from God. Consequently, when the saint comes to the third experience, the third feast of the faith, Tabernacles, the saint will know who he is for his identity is with Christ not with Adam and the sin nature. But the world, even other Christians, will not recognize his identity. The world did not recognize Jesus and the people of Israel, that household of the faith, did not know who He was either. For they looked on the outer and not the inner.

Perhaps another way to state the concept of unveiling is the usage of an affair that is currently done in the world today. When a famous artist or sculptor has finished his work it is transported to the location of the dedication and covered. On the appointed day people gather and with great anticipation strain to catch the first glimpse of this work of art as the curtain or veil is lifted off the piece of art. Thus, the people see a finished work and marvel at the piece and the handicraft of the artist.

You may have seen the *Pieta* sculptured by Michaelangelo. It is so magnificent. Smooth white marble I believe. Awe struck looking upon the piece it takes some time to begin to intimately discern the details like the curves, the eyes, the hands cradling the Lord, etc. Seeing the overview, the big picture overwhelms. Gradually, the details are seen when the "glare" of the first look is done. Michaelangelo had to see the *Pieta* in the rock before he could chisel the revelation.

Simeon proclaimed the "glare," the overview, of the Lord. Luke and others proclaimed the outworking, the manifestation, the revealing of the Lord on the intimate daily basis. So, when we look at the book of Revelation we must realize that the first verse is announcing the complete unveiling of the Lord to all who would read its pages.

1 Peter 1:5-7 uses the word "apocalypse" twice and is generally translated as "revealing." The apocalypse of Jesus Christ in these verses is <u>the faith</u> of the saint tried by fire. Christ was revealed in Daniel in the fire as the fourth man. This understanding also goes along with the book of Revelation in that the verses and chapters that follow 1:1 are designed to reveal the process which is necessary for the complete appreciation of the revelation of Jesus Christ.

Paul writes in Galatians 1:12 that the word that he received did not come "*from man, nor was I taught it, but it came through the revelation (apocalypse) of Jesus Christ.*" Paul as Saul had studied for years and was well acquainted with the Old Testament. But he knew not God. It takes an unveiling, the scales removed from your carnal mind, to know spiritual things. Knowledge does not make you spiritual although it could help your spiritual walk.

In Galatians 1:16 the word "revealed" in the KJV is the Greek word "apocalypse." So the translation could read: "When it pleased God to manifest in me..." or "appear in me...." The coming of the Lord is within a vessel during his lifetime. The apocalypse (The Revelation) is an allegorical book that is fulfilled within the individual.

The following reference study is quoted from J. Preston Eby: "The Greek word APOKALUPSIS is a derivative of APOKALUPTO. APOKALUPTO is a compound word composed of APO, meaning "off" or "away," and KALUPTO, meaning "to cover up." Thus APOKALUPSIS means to take the cover off, to uncover, unveil, reveal or disclose. It implies the drawing away or removal of everything that veils or hides, and therefore it is always opposed to concealment or secrecy, as in the following passage: "There is nothing covered that shall not be revealed (uncovered)" (Matt. 10:26). Our English word "revelation" has become for many a word that signifies a strange belief or some far-out doctrine, which should be handled as something delusive and dangerous, and avoided if possible. But this is just the opposite from the biblical meaning of the word, and the consideration we need to give to that which is revealed. That which is uncovered is no more a mystery, nor can it any longer be a threat. It is open to view, whether positive or negative, and can be considered without fear since it is no longer shrouded in darkness or mystery.

"In the following texts the word related to our Lord's appearing is from either the Greek APOKALUPSIS or APOKALUPTO. *"Even so shall it be in the day when the Son of man is REVEALED"* (Lk. 17:30). *"The sufferings of this present time are not worthy to be compared with the glory which shall be REVEALED in us"* (Row. 8:18). "So that ye come behind in no gift; waiting for the COMING (unveiling; revealment) of our Lord Jesus Christ" (I Cor.1:7). *"To you who are troubled rest with us, when the Lord Jesus shall be REVEALED from heaven...in flaming fire...when He shall come to be glorified in His saints"* (II Thes. 1:7-10). *"That the trial of your faith...might be found unto praise and honor and glory at the APPEARING of Jesus Christ"* (I Pet. 1:7). "Hope to the end for the grace that is to be brought unto you at the REVELATION of Jesus Christ" (I Pet. 1:13). *"Rejoice, in as much as ye are partakers of Christ's sufferings; that, when His glory shall be REVEALED, ye might be glad also with exceeding joy"* (I Pet. 4:13). *"The REVELATION of Jesus Christ ..."* (Rev. 1:1). *"For the earnest expectation of the creature waiteth for the MANIFESTATION (unveiling; revealment) of the sons of God"* (Rom. 8:19).

"Only by REVELATION, UNVEILING can we know the Christ of God or behold Him in His ineffable glory. When the light of the Holy Spirit shines in, the mists that have hung like a cloud over our minds, obscuring the King in His beauty, are cleared away. Then the realities which were once unseen become clearly visible and that which was once seen through a glass darkly is now seen face to face and that which was once known only in part is now known as we are known. The word "unveiling" is certainly the clearest possible translation of the word APOKALUPSIS. On the basis of this "unveiling" of our wonderful Christ, we may, then, expect the APOKALUPSIS to be understood not as a matter of His COMING, but merely of SEEING. It is not at all a question of our Lord making some change in location, as "coming" from high heaven back down into the atmosphere of this planet; it is, rather, the matter of Him who is already present with and within us becoming unveiled - uncovered disclosed, revealed in the power of the Holy Spirit that we may truly BEHOLD HIM in the fullness of Himself. It would be one thing for you to "feel a presence" in your room, but it would be something greater should that presence become visible, so that you SEE CLEARLY what was once veiled in obscurity.

"Since APOKALUPSIS means to reveal, or unveil, there must be something to unveil or which may be unveiled.

That something must be Present or it cannot be unveiled; and it must be hidden from sight or it cannot be disclosed. Jesus is PRESENT and that He is hidden from sight of the natural eye because "the Lord is that Spirit." We are now to find that His invisible presence, parousia is to be revealed, disclosed, uncovered, unveiled and that, too, to the whole world in due season. Are we looking for a so-called "second coming" of the Lord? Emphatically, we are NOT looking into the sky for such a thing BUT we most emphatically, are looking forward for the disclosure, uncovering, revealing of the Lord NOW PRESENT BUT HIDDEN in Spirit form. Truly the APOKALUPSIS of Jesus Christ is a yet future vision for the great mass of Christians as well as for the world, and to all of us there is yet much to be unveiled.

"*We greatly rejoice...that the trial of your faith...might be found unto praise and honor and glory at the appearing (apocalypse disclosure, uncovering, revelation, unveiling, manifestation) of Jesus Christ*" (I Pet. 1:6-7). Prayerful pondering of this scripture is all that is needed to grasp the meaning of the honor and glory that shall be ours, not in being caught up into the starry skies out of the trials which produce the honor and glory, nor in Jesus coming riding upon a cloud in the upper atmosphere, but when He is UNVEILED TO THE WHOLE WORLD IN HIS MANY-MEMBERED BODY OF SAINTS bringing deliverance to the entire groaning creation through the manifestation of His grace, glory and power which shall yet bring a larger measure of life and immortality to light through the gospel.

"Again, "*So that ye come behind in no gift, waiting for the coming (apokalupsis) of our Lord Jesus Christ*" (1 Cor. 1:7). We are waiting for the marvelous apokalupsis, disclosure, unveiling of Jesus Christ that which transcends

HIS GIFTS, wonderful as they are, as He manifests the fullness of the Son of God and His great, many-membered Christ body, but we are no longer gazing into the sky for His so-called "second coming" at some indefinite future date. Praise God, we are beholding the handiwork of our God on every hand today as He moves the nations like pawns on a chess board in mighty preparation for the closing events of this age and the ushering in of the more glorious age to come.

The great Italian sculptor, Benvenuto Cellini, told of receiving a block of marble with one flaw. Because of this flaw, no artist would submit a design - except one. In the public square of Florence a fence was built around that piece of marble, and a little shack was erected for the artist. For two years the sculptor labored. Then on a certain day a vast multitude of the citizens of Florence assembled in the public square; the fence was torn down, and the shack was taken away. At this unveiling all of Florence beheld the result and marveled. Since then, Italy and all the world has marveled at Michelangelo's "David." In that block of marble was a statue; others did not see it, but Michelangelo did. And, precious friend of mine, in the lump of clay which is you, the almighty Father sees an image too - the image of Jesus Christ! And God is working unceasingly and tirelessly to form the image of His Son in you. No truth has come with more soul-gripping force and power to the elect of the Lord than the beautiful hope of sonship to God. Well indeed may we yield ourselves into the hands of heaven's skilled sculptor that HE may form His Son in us, for the mind of omniscience has ordained that that sonship should be the HOPE OF ALL CREATION.

It is for sonship that the whole creation groans in a sort of universal travail while it eagerly waits to see the glorious sight of the sons of God coming into their own (Rom. 8:22-23)." unquote

Chapter Four

THE REVELATION OF THE TEMPLE

There is only one foundation upon which any truth can be built, and that foundation is Jesus, the Christ. For Christ is the Alpha, the first of all things. All things that were created were created through Him and exist through Him (John 1:3). Jesus Christ is the first and last of all things and thereby has preeminence over all.

Because He is the first of all creation, it is important that we realize that He was the first temple or house of God. For any man who has seen the Son has seen the Father. He was the express image of the invisible God. The Father was so well pleased with the manifestation of His Son that the Father placed His glory on His Son. As Christ did nothing save what would please the Father, we can easily see that He was the first and perfect example of what a temple would be.

When God said, "*Let there be light,*" we can rest assured that the light was created, and the very first manifestation of light was Jesus Christ Himself. He is the Light of the world which lightens every man who comes into the world. (John 1:9) All things were thereby created by that Light.

He was the first temple, and the temple was found where He was. That temple still exists because He is the ever present One who dwells in the heavens. It is a spiritual temple not made with hands. It appeared first in the heavens because that is where Christ first appeared. It was a considerable amount of time before Christ made His appearance on the earth plane. Why was His throne so far above the realms of the earth, heavens and time that these realms fled from before His presence (Rev. 20:11)?

In our understanding the Word of God declares in 1 Corinthians 15:46 that there is "first the natural; and afterward that which is spiritual." This understanding is true as far as understanding the ways of man, but Jesus was first Spirit and then lowered Himself to the earth realm (John 10:17, Heb. 2:7). God did dwell in Him bodily - in both His heavenly and earthly bodies. We who see through a glass darkly often see a blurred image and thereby interpret the Word of God poorly. However, He Who is the substance of all things sees through a clear glass because He is far above the earth realm.

His word of creation is still going on and the finished result will have all things pure and placed back into the Father of Lights. That first work, the first temple was none other than our Lord Jesus Christ. The Son of God is the firstborn of many brethren (Rom. 8:29). Many sons of God will be brought forth to deliver creation from the swamp of death and decay (Rom. 8:19). These sons seek to be delivered themselves from the bondage of corruption so that they might enter the glorious liberty of the heavenlies so that all creation might be delivered. Jesus as the model set aside the heavenlies and descended into our abyss of life to liberate us so that we might ascend and live before Him. Oh what good tidings He tells to Zion!

Accomplishing the perfect will of the Father, Jesus has ascended to His former state, but the fulfillment of His purpose shall be made manifest. The brethren that He has begotten, the sons of God, shall do His bidding. They will show on this earth plane the revelation of the fullness of the Godhead dwelling in them. Such is the grace of God Who has worked mightily in them, for they no longer exist in the sense of the carnal man but have been clothed upon with the tabernacle from above (2 Cor. 5:1).

The word "tabernacle" is similar in meaning to the word "temple." The first temple was the being of Jesus Christ. The number "two" in the Bible speaks of a witness, and another temple will appear to His glory. The Israelites foolishly thought that Christ was talking about the physical temple that they worshipped in when He said He was going to raise a temple on the third day. John 2:21 clearly shows that Jesus meant His body. All of Christendom knows and accepts that He was talking about His natural body being resurrected. The Lord was also talking about that Body of Christ which strives for perfection and is being raised up in the third day from when He spoke.

Christ was talking about a temple, but not one that could be built with hands. If we look at the word "temple" it means a physical building in Acts and is used twenty-four times. In 1 Corinthians 9:13 it also means a building, <u>But in every other book in the Bible it means a SPIRITUAL TEMPLE, a body, not a building</u>.

Christ said that He wanted to make His abode in us and that His Father would join Him (John 14:23, 17:21). As He is the temple of God, He desires that we also be the temple. This then is the second temple being formed as two is the number of witness. In Malachi it speaks of His coming quickly to the temple with a refiner's fire and fuller's soap. Truly, in these last days we see the coming of the Lord, and we proclaim the appearing of Christ in His temple, which temple ye are.

Jesus now is coming with the fire that was spoken about on the day of Pentecost. It is a fire to purify the sons of Levi, those called to be priests of the Kingdom (Rev. 1:6-7). It is a fire to purge away the old nature and to bake on the clay pot the final image that shall appear. It is with soap that the vessel is cleansed, being washed by the very Word of God, Christ Himself Who sits in the temple.

My friends, I would have you to know that no temple or physical building is going to be built in the natural city of Jerusalem. There is, however, a heavenly Jerusalem, which is the Bride of Christ (Rev. 21:9-11) and these shall be the temple of God. Having suffered with Him they shall also be glorified with Him (Rom. 8:17). Christ has called a people to be conformed to His image. These saints have set aside earthly ways, the ways of the fallen Adamic nature, and have put on the nature of Christ. In their ascending from the dust nature of the earth, they put on a heavenly body, even Christ. Yet, their aspiration shall not stop there, for they shall continue to ascend until they become like Him. These saints desire to have a spiritual temple fashioned after that of Christ's. It is a house not made with hands, for no man's nature is in the fashioning of it, as "hands" would suggest (2 Cor. 5:1). This new temple is totally accomplished by the nature of God dealing and working in the individual to do His good pleasure.

The word given to Abram was to forsake his country, kindred and even his father's house to go unto a land that the Lord would show him. Please read again Abram's call in Genesis 12. However, we soon find that Abram did not allow the Lord to run his temple. He obeyed Him at first when he left his country, but he took his kindred and his father with him. He forsook the old ways and former sins, but he kept the Adamic nature and the enemy close at hand.

Abram heard the word of God and believed the word of God but did not rightly divide the word of God. He was insistent on doing things the way HE heard the word and not specifically by what the Lord really said. Although he was the house or temple of God, he refused to allow God to BE the God of the temple.

Gradually we see his life changing because God's declaration will not return void without accomplishing what He desires. First we see in Abram's life that God causes his father to die. To us this represents that his desires had to be dealt with before he could go on with the Lord; his connection to the flesh had to die. Abram did not want to leave his father, but God in His infinite wisdom removed the father from Abram so that His will could be done in his life.

It is important to understand that Abram thought he was in the perfect will of God when he left the country. However he had not followed ALL of God's will. He had left the country, but he brought along some weights that beset him. With his father gone Abram needed to be separated from his nephew Lot. Lot speaks to us as a type of Satan, who no longer has a part of us when we become like Christ (Jn. 14:30). Once the old Adamic nature, his father, was removed, Lot had nothing he could touch in Abram.

Abram had continual trouble with Lot because Lot always chose the easier way. He chose the best ground, the easy flowing land in the valley that appealed to the eyes. Abram took the mountain land that speaks of the Rock.

Once Lot was separated from him Abram still was not fully delivered from his carnal understanding. God gave Abram another word about the coming of a son. Rather than letting God be his master, Abram tried to help things along by creating an Ishmael out of the flesh. The child of the flesh that was brought forth would continually hound and trouble the promised child.

While Abram became Bethel (Hebrew meaning: the house of God), he didn't allow God to be the ruler of the temple. Many are the saints who have received Christ, but they live their lives according to the dictates of their own mind as Abram did.

It took a lifetime for God to remove all vestiges of Abram's desires from him. It was 100 years before the child of the promise was born, 100 years of trials and tribulations before Abram could say that his desires were the Lord's.

As you know Abram was his name UNTIL it was changed to Abraham. Those called to sonship will no longer live to themselves but are the manifestation of Christ in the flesh - in the temple of God. Paul declared the same when he said, *"It is no longer I that liveth, but Christ that liveth in me"* (Gal. 2:20). Paul had died to self totally. His man of sin was revealed and dealt with. Paul fell away from all false pretenses and false coverings; he stripped them off until the God of all creation could be seen.

In this last day the temple of God is filled with all of His glory for all the earth will be filled with His glory. Death is swallowed up in the victory of His life. The Adamic nature does not exist. If we preach God has come, then we must see God in you and not Adam. We know God has come John 14:23 states He has made His abode in us, and the kingdom is within us (Luke 17:21).

Paul dethroned the captain of his soul, that fallen nature, and in its rightful place he allowed the Christ to come as the Day Star arising in his heart (2 Pet. 1:19). You see Paul allowed the man of sin to be revealed in order that he might be destroyed by the brightness of the Day Star. Abram and Jacob had name changes when they recognized their carnal natures and then gave the pre-eminence to Christ.

Many recognize their carnal natures but refuse to give the throne of their tabernacle over to God. Many verbally declare that God is on their throne, but the crucified life does not appear in them. When God truly sits on the throne of our heart He is like a refiner's fire. Christ comes suddenly to His temple when there are no obstacles to His kingship. The Lord's Prayer says that His kingdom is upon the earth; we are the earth and the kingdom is Within. (Luke 17:21). Yet it remains for that kingdom to be made manifest in the eyes of the earth dwellers.

God of the House of God will be seen. We as His temple manifest His nature in all realms, whether in, on or under the earth. For He shall receive glory in all the cosmos. (Phil. 2:10) Man shall be changed because it is in the plan and counsel of God, not because of man's doing. Just as God saw His Word to Abram fulfilled, whether Abram knew it or not, so too in this hour His Word shall be established. He is not slack concerning His promises, neither is He going to tarry. (2 Pet. 3:9, Hab. 2:3) The establishment of El Bethel (God of the House of God) can be seen in those who are giving true submission to the Lord's will.

"And there was given to me a reed like unto a rod and the angel stood, saying, rise, and measure the temple of God, and the altar and them that worship therein. But the court which is without the temple leave out, and measure it not..." Revelation 11:1-2

The rod and measurement speak of judgment. Amos (7:7-8) was told by the Lord, *"Behold, I am setting a plumb line in the midst of my people, Israel."* The word "measure" means to ascertain by a fixed standard. There is no other standard but Christ. But the Greek goes further and has implied in it that the measurement is allotted by rule, that is to say, that the measurement is done from a form of government standards, from a theocracy. Since we are called to rule and reign with Him, it is necessary that we be judged by the standards of His kingdom and not by our own understanding of His kingdom. Judgment always came on the people when they were disobedient. Many times the people were judged because the leadership was corrupt. So, here in Revelation 11 we find judgment is to begin at the house of the Lord. Is it caused by the leadership? Is it caused by the people themselves?

It is important to note that the judgment is not on the outercourt of the temple, which speaks of the natural body, but rather is upon the Holy Place and the Holy of Holies which speaks of the mind and the spirit. Another point to consider simultaneously is that the outercourt represents those in the realm of Passover or salvation. Why is there judgment in the Holy Place? The Holy Place represents the mind and the realm of Pentecost wherein the Holy Spirit leads the people.

The purpose that Jesus planned with His disciples before His resurrection was that the Holy Spirit would come (50 days later - penta) and baptize them with power so that the Spirit could lead them into all truth (John 16:13). Thus, the temple, you individually and the body of Christ corporately, is to be judged by the Holy Spirit. This judgment goes on in the mind, the Holy Place. It is a war because the carnal mind is at enmity against God, the mind of Christ. It is a war of Truth versus the depths of lies presented to us by the mind of the antichrist - that which is against, in place of Christ.

In the Old Testament if the high priest was cleansed, he went into the Holy Place and could try to go into the Holy of Holies. But if his mind was not of the Lord, he would die before he could enter the Holy of Holies, even as Nadab and Abihu who offered unholy fire before the Lord at the altar of incense. Note that they were cleansed to enter in, i.e. had the mind of God (Christ) to be in the Holy Place, but were not led of the Spirit but rather the flesh and offered that which was unholy. Thus, they were consumed.

It is important to note that the death of these two is important to us today. For their death created an opportunity for us to see that one could have the mind of Christ and still not be led by the Spirit! As an example, suppose that you know a person who is committing adultery. You know from scripture that it is sinful to do that. You have the mind of Christ on that, the understanding. But if you are not led by the Spirit in how you approach the person, you are in the flesh - sinful. You proceed to chastise the person from a correct understanding but without the wisdom of God how to do it and without the manner of restoration. Consequently, you like the others will be consumed.

It is only those who are led by the Spirit that are the sons of God (Romans 8:14). Jesus obviously had the mind of Christ. But let me say that He never used it. He only did what He saw His Father in heaven do (John 5:19, 30). Jesus was led at all times by the Spirit and never yielded to just the use of His mind. The church system of leadership has used their mind. The people are taught truth, and then each denomination builds a camp around the truth and states there is no other truth. Baptists, in general, preach a great word of salvation by grace. But let a Pentecostal speak of another experience in the Lord - the baptism of the Holy Spirit - and the Baptist cries out that it is of the devil. The Pentecostals camp around their experience and deny that there is a third - Tabernacles. And on and on it goes. Truth becomes a thing rather than a relationship with Him who is Truth.

The importance of growth in God is that each denomination has a portion of Him in their understanding, but judgment must begin on these denominations because they fail to be led of the Spirit and are just led by the righteous understanding of their mind. But can we condemn these denominations that are made up of people? For it is the individual who has that mindset which brings about these systems. God is judging the church - you and I - individually. He is removing out of our minds that which is divisive from His nature.

Consequently, many of the churches have a migration going on. People leaving the old more staid denominations for the more evangelical, while some from the more evangelical are moving on seeking a deeper walk. This is God's plan. *"For He would that none would perish, and He is the Savior of all men especially those that believe"* (1 Timothy 4:10). He judges us by revealing to us that we are not moving in all of His nature which He has already given us. For it brings glory and praise to Him not by the things that we do but by the revelation of Himself in us. Since we are His temple, He wishes to be seen in us.

The judgment is brought to the house, the temple (individually and corporately) by an angel the verse states. Angels are covered in detail elsewhere in this book . But suffice it to say that this can be a corporate or individual bringing forth this word. The word "**angel**" means a messenger, one who brings good news. It is not often that when judgment comes people think of it as good news. But it is because it holds us accountable to the standard of Christ and being conformed to His image.

"Then the temple of God was opened in heaven and the ark of the covenant was seen in His temple, and there were lightnings, noises, thunderings, an earthquake and great hail." Revelation 11:19

The word "temple" here, as in all cases in the book of Revelation is the Greek word "naos" which is used in conjunction with 1 Corinthians 3:16-17 that states your body is the temple of the Holy Spirit. So, your "body" was opened in heaven. What does that mean?

First, realize that when you are born again and come to the realization that Christ Jesus is your personal Savior, you are no longer a temple for carnal abuse, but have been transformed by the renewing of your mind (Romans 12:2) and translated into the kingdom of God (Colossians 1:13). Thus, your body becomes the habitation of God (John 14:23). No longer an earthly being (made of Adam who was made of the dust), you are now a heavenly creation. Consequently, your temple is joined with, has become one with heaven.

This concept is difficult for saints to grasp. They feel because of various reasons or their religious training, that their body is ugly, cannot be godly, is aging and if it were godly it wouldn't age, etc. All these thoughts and more are not pertinent to the truth. For the house that we talk about is the house of 2 Corinthians 5. It is a house not made with hands, eternal, in heaven. We know that if this earthly house is dissolved (see 2 Peter 3:10), that the heavenly one is revealed.

<u>Our temple is not made of dust; it is not the Adamic temple</u>. It is the spiritual house that God is building in us. This spiritual house (a house within a house) becomes one with heaven. As one looks on the transfiguration of Christ in Matthew 17:2, the Wuest translation reads: "And the manner of His outward expression was changed before them, that expression coming from and being representative of His inner being." The truth here is that God can at any time change the outer by the life of the inner. The saint looks on the outer and thinks it is the inner. Carnal man that thou art.

Consider 1 Corinthians 6:17 which states *"that he that is joined to the Lord is one Spirit."* This is a marriage relationship. It is a joining of spirit, soul and body. This union causes the temple to be elevated into heaven, which is not a natural place but a spiritual one. Paul was so in union with God that whether in the body or not he did not know, but he was caught up to paradise (2 Corinthians 13). Such a place is a realm of life wherein there is no devil that can touch you.

When you have experienced the feast of Tabernacles, that time of union, you begin to walk in heavenly places and you can recognize that you dwell there (Rev. 12:12). The purpose of being in the heavenly realm is so that God can open you up that others can see Whom you have possessed - Christ. Then they can be attracted to Him.

"Mercy and truth have met together, righteousness and peace have kissed each other." (Psalm 85:10) When heaven and earth become one, such occurs. This is what happens in Revelation 11:19. The spirit and soul have been married and become one. For Adam was a living soul (Genesis 2:7) until he died (Ezekiel 18:4). But being quickened, vivified, made alive by God in the regeneration through our Savior, who made His soul an offering for ours (Isaiah 53:10), we can experience the soul and spirit becoming one. Effectively, this causes the birthing of the manchild in Revelation 12.

So, when heaven and earth are joined together, this speaks of the inner man and the outer becoming one; it speaks of the spirit and the soul becoming one; it speaks of God Who sits in our temple becoming one with us. Oh, the temple was opened in heaven! I cannot proclaim on the written page the depth of the revelation of Him in this.

Revelation 11:19 says the temple was opened, joined with, in union with heaven. Where is heaven? Has not the Lord said that He would make His abode in us (John 14:20, 23)? Is not the Kingdom of God within (Luke 17:21)? Thus, the body of the vessel (you) is to reveal the fullness of God (John 1:16, Eph. 1:23, Col. 1:9, 2:9). Especially so since our life is hid with God in Christ!

"The ark of the testimony was seen in heaven," Revelation 11:19 states. Some background information might be appropriate to grasp the full understanding of what is being said. The word "testimony" is derived from "testis" a Latin word. We also derive from "testis" legal terms in English.

But further study will reveal that "testis" also is part of the word testicle. The testicle of the man provides the semen to produce life. In Genesis the King James Version states that Jacob swore by his thigh (Genesis 24:2 see also Genesis 47:29). The implication here is he swore by that which gave life and if he were wrong, he might lose an appendage. I have been told that before the Bible was used to swear by in court cases that it was common in English society that the man would swear by his testicles, literally grab them and swore that his oath would be true or he would forfeit the ability to produce life again. We are the ark and He is the testimony. He is the issuer of life from within us seeking to place the incorruptible seed in all creation.

So, the ark of the testimony was opened in heaven. The source of life. Passover (salvation experience) and Pentecost (baptism of the Holy Spirit) are established by the feast of Tabernacles which proceeds from the ark of the covenant in the life realm. In Ezekiel we see water issuing forth from underneath the ark and wherever it goes, it brings life eternal. God's glory dwelt in the Holy of Holies which is represented by the feast of Tabernacles.

The issues of life proceed from the throne of God. An incorruptible seed (2 Peter 1:23) that has been placed within each vessel will develop the divine nature (2 Peter 1:4), that house within a house (2 Corinthians 5). God can give life and it only. We are to be the ark, the carrier of the seed issued from God Who is within us. We are to be the fruit of the Spirit, the issue of life. Oh, that we, too, would become fathers, producing the way of the Spirit. This is the testimony that causes the woman of Revelation 12 (the church which is the bride of Christ, or in the natural - your soul) to receive the seed from the Spirit of Christ and produce an offspring.

It takes the masculine, the Spirit, to penetrate the soul, the feminine. It is the soul that receives the mind of Christ and is renewed daily after the inner man. Growth within will cause the manifestation of the nature of God to be seen outwardly, even as Jesus was transfigured and his inner nature was revealed outwardly.

Paul mentions in Hebrews 9:4 that there were three things in the original ark of the covenant: Aaron's rod that budded, the two tablets which contained the ten commandments and the earthen jar overlaid with gold which had hid in it the manna from the wilderness. David brought the ark back to Israel (1 Chronicles 15). Solomon set the ark in the temple and removed its staves (1 Kings 8) which signifies that you as the temple are the final resting place for the Lord and He will speak to all from in the Holy of Holies which is within. But 1 Kings 8:9 states that there was only one thing in the ark - the two stones.

The significance of this must not be lost. If you remember your Bible stories you know how all twelve tribes wanted to be the mouthpiece for the Lord and complained to Moses. So they cast lots by using their shepherd's staffs. The staff was the bread of life to the sheep because it was the staff that saved them from a cliff. It was the staff that withstood the lion, the bear and the wolf. The one staff God chose bloomed. This told the leaders of each tribe that God had chosen Aaron.

Well, in the ark of the temple there is no Aaron's rod. There is no "man" ministry. The time of the Adamic ministry is over. Only the Christ nature can come forth to establish the life of God. It is the manifestation of the new creation man within who is breaking out all over and removing the fallen nature, that man of sin.

As is also noted the hidden manna of the earthen jar overlaid with gold is missing. Why? The earthen jar speaks of the Adamic man made of dust. The overlay of gold speaks of the divinity of God, the glory of God, placed on Adam. The manna which in Hebrew means: "What is it?", is no longer hidden. The nature of Christ is revealed, broken forth out of the carnal vessel in which it was deposited. Light was hid in a dark place! But no more.

The ten commandments remain. The church system has taught us the ten commandments as a legalistic truth - do not commit adultery, do not lie, etc. Each of these are impossible to keep in our own self-effort. Saints try and fail. Condemnation follows. <u>The ten commandments are not to be kept but to be lived!</u> Oh, the truth of that is so important that God left the two stones in the ark. The word they express is eternal, life giving, never ending. Remember the life found in the ten commandments was so great that Moses' face shown. But even more than that, Moses spoke to his brother Aaron and he received life too. It was God who took Aaron. It was God who took Moses' life - and his life forces were not abated! He did not age because the ten commandments, the very nature of God Himself, was so worked into the fiber of Moses that he could not die! Ponder that life. The ten commandments are not a legalistic set of rules but a lifestyle that one enters into and a lifestyle that can change you.

"...He that is begotten of God <u>keeps himself</u> and the <u>wicked one touches him not</u>" (1 John 5:18). *"He that is begotten of God, which we are through Christ Jesus, does not sin"* (1 John 3:6, 9, 5:18). When one enters into union with God, it is not in your consciousness to sin. Adam desires to sin, looks to sin and will sin. You know that you dwell in Adam if those occur in you. But if you are begotten from above, entered into the feast of Tabernacles, are in union with Him, there is no desire to sin. In fact, when faced with the test of sin in your wilderness, you like Christ rise up and proclaim who you are. You identify with God and God's interpretation of life and not the ways of Adam or the flesh.

The ten commandments are life. Do not commit adultery is not a struggle but rather a simple walk because there is no desire to follow such a path. Jesus stated that Satan came and could not find anything in Him (John 14:30), and we can walk even as He walked (1 John 2:6) because we have been freed from the law of sin and death (Romans 6:14,18). When one enters into union with God, the ability to live beyond the desires of the flesh is a reality.

Truly understanding marriage scripturally and spiritually will eliminate any contemplation of adultery. Truly understanding God removes the carnal desire to set yourself up as God. And on it goes for each of the commandments. His words are life. Jesus said the ten could be summed up in two.

Luke 10:27 states: *"Thou shalt love the Lord your God with all your heart, and with all your soul, and with all your strength and with all your mind; and your neighbor as yourself."* If this be true, then 1 John 4:20 must also be considered - *"...he that loves not his brother whom he has seen, how can he love God whom he has not seen?"* Keeping yourself means to remain in the love of God and in so doing fulfill the law.

The ten commandments remain in the ark of the testimony because they are life unto our bones. Jesus told the lawyer who came to him that if the lawyer kept the commandments they would be life unto him (Luke 10:28). Only life resides in the ark realm. <u>Remember you are the ark; Christ in you is the testimony</u>.

"...and there were lightnings, and voices, and thunderings, and an earthquake, and great hail" (Revelation 11:19b)

Lightning is caused by positive ions in the heavens coming in contact with negative ions of the earth. The air becomes stratified because of the electrical charges and then thunder follows the lightning. Sometimes the cloud is negative and the positive earth responds to make the connection. Thunder is caused by the heating of the earth which causes unstable air/moisture to occur. Eventually this causes thunder.

Lightning from heaven is found in Matthew 24:27 which states: *"For as the lightning comes out of the east, shines even unto the west, so also shall the coming of the Son of Man be."* Symbolically, the rapid manifestation of the Son of Man is compared to lightning. The appearance of Christ in the sons of God (Romans 8:19) is a corporate manifestation at the same time in many. As the lightning is seen in heaven around the ark of the testimony, it speaks of the glory cloud of day and the fire by night in the wilderness as a testimony of the Lord being with His people. The lightning speaks of the birth of the manchild also (Revelation 12). Your salvation shall break forth speedily and the righteousness shall go before you; the glory of the Lord...(Isaiah 58:8). For He is the Light in us coming forth, raising us up never to dwell in the earth again but to live in the heavens (Revelation 12:12, 1 Corinthians 15:49).

Where Rev.11:19 states the plural of lightning, voice, thunder, the verse only expresses a singular of earthquake. The earth that is quaking is directly related to the next chapter and the woman who is about to give birth. Some have said it was Mary giving birth to Christ. The woman represents the church birthing the sons of God. On an individual basis it represents the saint giving birth to Christ Who is manifested through that individual.

The earth quaking is the Adamic nature, that dead dust, which gives up its dead. These have been led from Adam's captivity and are now captive to the Lord. The earth quakes and that which is of Him is revealed while all else is removed. "*Awake (resurrect), awake, put on thy strength O Zion; put on thy beautiful garments, O Jerusalem, the holy city; for henceforth there shall no more come into thee the uncircumcised and the unclean. Shake thyself from the dust, arise and sit down...*" (Isaiah 52:1-2). Realizing who we are because of the blood of Christ, we need to put on our strength, our beautiful garment which is none other than the garment of light we had before the fall. Let us shed these "skins" given after the fall by the Lord (Genesis 3:21). Only those circumcised by the Cherubim of the garden with the flaming sword can enter in - enter into the arena of life wherein the Cherubim dwell, move and have their being - Tabernacles.

We note there are three steps: Shake. Arise. Sit down. The grammar structure is plain. We must shake ourselves from the dust and examine ourselves to see whether we truly be in the faith. Then we must arise or resurrect from the flesh plane, that carnal corruption of the mind. Then we can sit with Him in heavenly places having entered into union and allow Him to come forth and finish the work that was begun in the Spirit.

Jesus was buried in the Garden (John 19:41) even as Adam died in the garden of Eden. Life always comes out of the tomb experience. It is only when we are dead to sin and freed from the Adamic nature by identifying with the Life of Christ that we can break forth from the dead carcass we are in and fly like a butterfly coming forth from its chrysalis. This is a major earthquake. The earthquake of Revelation 11:19 is that of life coming forth from the realm of death. The heavenly man is making his appearance as he descends from the heaven with a shout of affirmation to be seen on the earth. He comes forth and walks on the earth because the serpent has been placed under His feet even as the serpent was placed under Christ's. The birth of the sons of God is the beginning of the fulfillment of the prophecy to Eve in Genesis 3:16 where she will bring deliverance through childbearing.

The earth always quakes when one grasps the life found in the ten commandments. For if one lives in the commandments even as Jesus did, true power and life are made evident as a sign and testimony to the people who have not attained. While it was God's plan to offer His Son as a sacrifice for our sins, the manifestation of Life by Him disturbed the people, especially the religious ones who had Him killed. The manifestation of Life always destroys the yoke of death.

At the time of Jesus, Rome ruled the earth. They prescribed the religion of worshipping the Emperor as a god. When the Christians refused to bow to the dictates of the government, the state had two courses of action: remove the impediment to their power or ignore them. Since the Christians were so large a group and growing fast, the state decided to eliminate them through lions, burnings etc.

When the state decided to do this, the state immediately acknowledged that there was a higher power than itself. For if what the Christians were doing was false the state had nothing to fear. But if it were true, Rome had to maintain its power base. The Christians by not bowing actually destroyed the state of Rome then immediately. The Christians did destroy the Roman Empire by denying the power of Rome. The faith increased daily and eventually Rome fell. But when you have life it gives you power over the circumstance. Jesus told Pilate to do what he had to do, but Jesus also let Pilate know that Pilate could not do anything without Christ's okay. That is the revelation of the ultimate power. As one develops in the realm of Tabernacles, that place of union with God, his temple begins to manifest a change. It is quickened, vivified by the changes. What changes? Not natural changes but like Jesus you being to speak as one with authority that people have not heard before (Matthew 7:29). This power, this authority, which is of Christ radiates from you and causes people to react. When the brethren learn to be proactive they shall overthrow all principalities and powers.

Our testimony is Christ. As He was able to fulfill the ten commandments because He lived in the Life of them, so too we. As we identify with His death, we are identified with His life. This correct identification removes sin, which in the Greek is "hamartia" which means "missing the mark." We are to be His ensign, even as He was a sign to a perverse generation (Matthew 12 39. Mark 8:12, 1 Corinthians 1 22). The temple of the individual, as well as the corporate body of Christ is the sign, the manifestation of Him unto the world.

"And I looked and behold a white cloud, and upon the cloud *one* sat like unto the son of man, having on his head a golden crown and in his hand a sharp sickle. And another angel came out of the temple, crying with a loud voice to him that sat on the cloud, thrust in thy sickle, and reap; for the time is come for you to reap; for the harvest of the earth is ripe.....And another angel came out of the temple which is in heaven, he also having a sharp sickle." Revelation 14:14-17

In these verse we see that the angel comes out of the temple proclaiming to "one who sat on the cloud." The word "one" is italicized in the KJV and is not found in the Greek but implied. A good study in the book of Revelation is "like unto" and "one" because every time it refers to the corporate body of Christ. It seems to imply with study the "one" is referring to the group, or corporate expression of Christ. The importance of this verse and what is said is directly related to the one that sat on the cloud. The cloud that the "one" is found in is the cloud of witnesses, the other saints who have entered into union with God over all the ages. *"For he who is joined to the Lord is one Spirit"* the scripture states and that does not just mean in our natural lifetime only because when one is joined with God He is the I AM, and past and future are found in Him as God of the Living.

Revelation 1:13 and 4:2 both deal with those who have been called out from within the church to become the body of Christ upon which He can lay His head. All of chapter 14 deals with the corporate body of Christ and the corporate manifestation of Christ expressed through His body. Let me state that again. All that is discussed in Chapter 14 is manifested through the body of Christ - saints individually and corporately.

Out of the temple, out of the body comes the angelic ministry. I know that you have seen such occur. First, our pattern, Jesus Christ, revealed it on the Mount of Transfiguration. Wuest brings it out in his translation in this way: "And the manner of Christ's inward nature became His outward expression." The transfiguration was the nature of Christ emanating through the flesh of His body. Such is the case when the angel comes out of the temple. It is that inward nature of the heavenly government, the kingdom of God that comes through the person.

How often we have seen the hand of God moving. A person needs uplifting and then life is ministered to the person. This is a form of the angelic ministry. For as one identifies with the Lord and your life is hid in Him, you become His manifestation in the world. Who harvests the world? Is it angels or people like yourself who lead others to the Lord for salvation. There is neither male nor female in Christ, Paul writes in Galatians. That is an angelic ministry from the kingdom. Not that the natural is done away, but when one enters the kingdom, divisions do not exist. Life is ministered from the heavenly realm and not from the natural.

As one reads on in Revelation 14:18 we see that the vine is to be trampled. Remember 11:2 states that the outercourt is to be judged by the Gentiles. This body, that outercourt, the church of the outercourt (saved but not empowered by the Holy Spirit) is harvested by an angelic ministry. They are trampled outside the city, even as Christ was killed outside the camp. A goodly pattern here. For the ministry of life requires as Paul states: *"But in all things approving ourselves as ministers of God: in much patience, in tribulations, in needs, in distress, in stripes, in imprisonments, in tumults, in labor..."* (2 Corinthians 6:4-7) *"We are hard pressed on every side, yet not crushed; we are perplexed but not in despair; persecuted but not forsaken; struck down but not destroyed - always carrying about in the body the dying of the Lord Jesus, that the life of Jesus may also be manifested in our body."* (2 Corinthians 4:8-10).

It is the purpose of God that the church, the outercourt expression or individually - the person's body, be a vessel sown for the glory of God. In the early church, lions ate some saints. In the middle ages the Catholics under the Popes persecuted the brethren through burnings at the stake, beds of nails, etc. (read <u>Foxe's Book of Martyrs</u>). But to those who lay down their bodies as seeds for the kingdom, the results are fortuitous.

The message of these angels or a divine messengers who bring the "evangel or good news" is that life from the throne room is a fire which causes people to be first harvested. They are harvested into life or into judgment so that they will chose life after death is worked out of them.

"And the seven angels came out of the temple, having the seven plagues, clothed in pure and white linen, and having their breasts girded with golden girdles... and the temple was filled with smoke from the glory of God, and from His power; and no man was able to enter into the temple, til the seven plagues of the seven angels were fulfilled." Revelation 15:6-8

In the Old Testament the Holy of Holies was filled with the glory cloud of God (Exodus 40:34). The Tabernacle had the cloud above the Mercy Seat (Leviticus 16:2). We find also that the cloud filled Solomon's Temple (1 Kings 8:10). In Revelation 15 we find the word "smoke" is analogous to the cloud. The angelic ministry comes out of the cloud of His nature. Thus, the angelic ministry is Spirit-led from the Holy of Holies to reach out of the vessel into another vessel, person. Again the messenger is an angel, one with a message of good news.

How are seven plagues good news? Seven in the scriptures is a number that represents completion. So the plagues finish in totality what they are supposed to accomplish. Next the plagues are ministered by angels, saints of the Most High. These saints come not in judgment unto death but unto life. The dealings are a plague for the Adamic nature that resides in the realm of death, but the vessels bringing the plague do so in order that the individual might be redeemed from the Adamic fallen nature. It is interesting to note that the Word of God is sharper than any two edged sword unto the Christian, but it is a sickle unto those who live after the body, the flesh.

"No man" was able to enter the temple. That means that no Adamic, fallen nature can put on the nature of God. That means there is no carnal nature that can be revealed in the temple. Just as the two priests were killed for entering into the temple in an unholy manner, so this means that those who enter in are holy because "no man" will be able to enter.

These angels had golden girdles around their breasts. This is similar to Revelation 1:13 where there is "one like unto the Son of Man." While we will discuss that later, suffice it to say that the corporate body of Christ has golden girdles around their breasts. The angels are part of that body of Christ who are the ministers of God in this life. The gold speaks of the divine nature of God. The paps speak of the El

Shaddai, the full breasted one, the one who gives milk, the basis of life. Thus, these who have their chest girded with gold have the purity of the gospel within them and are ready to give suckle to those who need to be fed.

These angels will feed the milk of the word of God unto those who are in that stage in their lives. When we get saved God moves plagues on us to remove from us those things which hinder, and these plagues bring life because of the release they cause. Many are the testimonies that people get saved and their desires for liquor or cigarettes leave. The plague of God is unto life, and the milk of the word so engulfs us that we are able to cast off those weights that beset us. Thank God for the purity of the milk of the word that frees us from the law of sin and death.

These angels are clothed in pure white linen. Linen is different than wool. Wool speaks of sweat and self-effort. Linen speaks of refinement and freshness without sweat. Thus, the thought expressed here is that the effort of the Spirit-led life is effortless, that is, it is free of the contrivances of the carnal mind. Being led of the Spirit, this angelic ministry of the kingdom is not hindered by the death throes of man. Jesus was not hindered by the natural world nor the kingdoms of this world. These angels are not hindered either. The purity of their word and the life they possess empowers the deliverance that they provide.

So, from out of your midst shall come a revelation of an angel. But this is larger than that. For there shall come <u>angels plural</u> out of the temple. This means that those, who like Paul have entered into a realm of the Spirit, see and are encouraged by a cloud of witnesses beyond the veil who support and enhance the ministry of the one who remains on the earth. In another sense, if the reader can prayerfully hear, the rest of the body of Christ can flow through you if you have rightly discerned the body of Christ. For as the bruised toe tells the brain or as the burned finger tells the brain, so the temple ministry is to each member of the body. For the temple ministry of angels brings its wisdom for the healing of the toe and the finger. Yet, each has to flow and communicate with the other.

John 7:37 is a message unto itself. One river or rivers? One vessel many rivers is what it states. Out of your temple come angels. Out of your body flow rivers. It is one in the same. He that is joined to the Lord is one Spirit. Thus, those individuals who are joined to Him are thereby joined to each other and can flow through each other because of Him. In my weakness, you can become my strength!

"And I heard a great voice out of the temple saying to the seven angels, go your ways, and pour out your vials of wrath of God upon the earth ....and the seventh angel poured out his vial into the air; and there came a great voice out of the temple of heaven, from the throne, saying it is done." Revelation 16:1,17

The Lord resides in us. He has come and made his abode in us (John 14:20, 23). So He speaks out of the vessel because "heaven" is in us - it is not external. God speaks out of us that it is "done." What is done? The purpose of the vials is accomplished. What is that purpose? It is not a judgment unto death because Paul states: "O death where is thy sting? O grave, where is your victory?" (1 Corinthians 15:56). It is a judgment unto life.

If I can be so bold as to state that the book of Revelation may be located at the end of the Bible but it is not the "last word." For the book of Revelation deals with the struggle of the saint to reveal Christ. It does not deal with the "unsaved" or the "world" and their total result. We have been wrongly taught that Revelation is about the end of the world. I would declare that it is about the full revelation of Christ in His body that all the world would see it and become saved. However, 1 Corinthians 15:22-28 reveals that as Adam brought death to all, so in Christ shall all be made alive. In fact, it goes further for clarification in verse 28 and states: *"Now when all things are made subject to Him (i.e. Jesus), then the Son Himself will also be subject to Him (i.e. God) Who put all things under Him <u>that God may be all in all.</u>"*

It is done when the saints of God are redeemed from the earth, that Adamic man who was made of the earth. When the church fully reveals the nature of Christ in their own person and then corporately, the world will come to them seeking Him whom they reveal.

Jesus cried, *"It is finished."* He finished the work of grace and forgiveness our very salvation. Those conformed to His image are the full revelation of the complete work of grace as He is revealed in a people. When the sons of God are manifested, the firstfruits of a new creation, He will say "It is finished" for the redemption has occurred. The manifestation of life in a people will draw all men unto Him.

"And I saw no temple therein, for the Lord God Almighty and the Lamb are the temple of it." Revelation 21:22

There was found no temple in the New Jerusalem. The New Jerusalem is not a literal city as some have taught. It is allegorical. Revelation interprets itself many times. In 21:9-10 it reads: *"...Come, I will show you the Lamb's wife. And he carried me away in the Spirit ....and showed me... Jerusalem."* This is not a physical, literal city, but is the Lamb's wife. The Lamb is Christ and the wife is the bride which is the church. Paul even writes in Hebrews 12:22 that Jerusalem is the general assembly of the church.

Now that we know that Jerusalem is the bride of Christ, why then is there no need for a temple? The reason there is no temple in the city is that there is no need for a temple, since your body is the temple of the Holy Spirit. Each saint who individually is married to Christ as well as corporately is a part of the bride or the church. Therefore, the physical body of the individual will be full of light - the manifestation of Him coming or being revealed in the vessel. This will be done in many. For the Lord God and the Lamb are the temple in the city. What greater joy could there be than to have the Lord fully made manifest in your life? What could be a better way to be a temple of God? This is the purpose of the book of Revelation. The book of Revelation shows the end result - Christ in you the hope of glory.

Revelation 3:12 states that the person is a pillar in the temple of God if he overcomes. What is written on the vessel is the name of God, the name of the city of God and God's new name. When one enters into the feast of Tabernacles, the life/union with God causes a tremendous change in the outlook of the individual. For now you see yourself more as part of the corporate (i.e. pillar of God in the temple) and less as an individual. Therefore your pleasure is to rejoice in being a part of the plan of God instead of being the plan of God. Tabernacles is a corporate "thing" accomplished through individuals who have rescinded their rights.

Adam didn't fall in a literal sense, but fell spiritually. He lost his temple and was covered with a garment of skin. He who was the lightbearer, Lucifer, was encompassed with darkness and the light hid within. But blessed be the Lord God Almighty who has moved on our behalf and has raised us from the grave, leaving behind the old garment that we might be clothed upon with an eternal house made in the heavens (2 Corinthians 5 - see our tape). He has delivered us, translated us from the Adamic realm into the heavenly that we might be joint-heirs with Him in life.

Know ye not that your body is the temple of the Holy Spirit? Do you comprehend that verse's depth of meaning? For if it is true, you are holy, undefiled because you keep yourself from the desires of the flesh because of the life of God working within you. If the desires of the flesh are strong rivers in you then there is a need to move closer to the life of God within which will dry up that muddy river of Adamic flesh.

Yet, that understanding of knowing you are the temple, as great as it is, pales in the wake of the One who is the temple of the city! He is the light within that is bursting forth on the earth plane today. It is He in the midst of you. It is He who lifts you out of living in the hope of the future or the dregs of the past and puts you in the I AM. It is He who has come suddenly to His temple and placed His glory there (2 Thess. 1:10).

To know that you are in union with Him and have accepted His name as your last name so that your identity is lost in your manifestation of His name, this is life. Where He is, there is no sorrow, no war, no enemy, etc. When you come to the realization that your life is hid in God and that He is the temple in which you live, what a joy there is.

The joy in knowing you are the temple is nothing to be compared to realizing that He is the revelation of the temple, He is found in a corporate expression, and He is seen in you, one brick of the corporately expressed temple.

Chapter Five

ANGELS

The surety of a better covenant than that of Aaron and the sacrifices of the Old Testament was Christ Jesus. He came not out of the loins of a man but from heaven itself. He was a heavenly man and we must bear the image of Him (1 Corinthians 15:47-49). As Cassirer states in his translation of Hebrews 8:2-4 "... *one who in performing his ministry in the sanctuary...if he were on earth would not be a priest at all.*" The man whom we know as our Savior was a heavenly man, a spiritual man. He was not of Adam's descent or lineage, although it appears so from the natural side. For He was not natural. Born of a woman, yes indeed. But He did not come from a woman, nor did He come from Adam. He is the great I AM.

What then is an angel? The word itself comes from the Greek meaning a messenger. In fact, its derivation seems to be related to the words apostle, evangel and evangelist. Apostle is a sent one with a divine message and evangel means a message of good news from another order. Christ, who came after the order of Melchizedek which ministry is referred to in Hebrews 9:11, states "....*which does not belong to this order of creation at all.* " (Cassirer's God's New Covenant, A New Testament Translation)

Understanding angels in the book of Revelation is very important. When the word "angel" is used the individual because of the painters of the Middle Ages immediately envisions a cherubic creature, a small child with wings, or perhaps an adult in a white robe with wings. This religious picture formed in our mind is so strong that it is difficult not to believe what we have been taught. Yet there seems to be some concern that the religious teachings that we have received are not the absolute truth. The Bible interprets itself quite well.

Careful study of the Bible itself will reveal that the angels mentioned in the Holy Scriptures are far different from what we have previously conceived in our carnal religious mind. Paul was an apostle *"not from men nor through man."* His ministry was divinely inspired.

Apostles are, because of their position in the government of God, angelic, that is divine messengers of a better covenant. Consider what Paul writes in Galatians 4:14: "....***but you received me as an angel of God****, even as Christ Jesus.*" This verse of scripture is inspired of the Holy Spirit. It must be a true statement. Notice that Paul did not say "Jesus Christ." There was only one man who was our Savior. But Paul did say that he was received as "Christ Jesus." This is legitimate because the phrase "Christ Jesus" refers to the ascended Lord who has returned and inhabited our hearts via the Holy Spirit (John 20:17, 14:16-18, Acts 2:4).

Angels are not ethereal, intangible, vaporous things, but can be handled, touched, seen of men and still made of flesh like you and I have. Paul was definitely "other worldly" but he was one of us. Consider the following verse: *"Then he measured its wall: one hundred and forty-four cubits, according to the **measure of a man**, that is, **of an angel**."* Revelation 21:17 NKJV Here we find that the Scripture declares again that an angel is equated with a man. This verse clearly resembles in its truth the truth found in Galatians 4:14 - angels are men, human beings. Scripture interprets itself.

There is no doubt with other translations that such a truth is expressed. The Amplified Bible agrees, the Diaglott agrees, as does Moffat's, Young's and others. Yet, religious teaching has expressed to us over the years that angels are non - human, winged entities. The Greek does not express any indication that an angel is a winged creature. Scripture seems to indicate otherwise.

Revelation 21:16 states that the "city" was square. The cube was the symbol of perfection. Both Plato and Aristotle refer to the fact that in Greece the good man was called "four-square" (Plato, Protagoras 339 B; Aristotle, Nicomachean Ethics 1. 10. 11 ; Rhetoric 3.11). There is no doubt of the symbolism which John intends. Thus, the concept that John was writing from was that a man was "square" and we know that the "city" of Revelation 21 is not literal for 21:9-10 states: *"..Come, I will show you the bride, the Lamb's wife* (the church Ephesians 5:25-26).... *and showed me the great city, the holy Jerusalem."* John was trying to speak to the church about spiritual things that will occur in a people. But carnal man has interpreted apocryphal truth with fallacious premises.

GABRIEL

Gabriel, an angel, appears in Daniel 9:20-27 and also in Luke 1:26-38. The first occurrence as well as the second deals with the coming of the Lord. The announcements spanned centuries. Each were prophetic. The first was proclaiming the appearing of Christ as well as prophesying even passed the time of the manifestation of the Son of God in the flesh. The second not only deals with the immediate coming of Jesus but also of His future role as well. It is believed that Gabriel also was the angel that spoke to the shepherds (Luke 2:13).

Yet, this man Gabriel was not a 600 year old angel (Daniel was estimated to be written about 600 BC) that reappeared at the time of Christ, as some would propose. Perhaps the most interesting point about Gabriel is that of Daniel 9:21 which states: "*even the man Gabriel.*" This clearly reveals that Gabriel was a man AND also was an angel. As we know, no man has ever lived over 175 years of age since Abraham.

First, we need to understand that the spanning of the centuries would imply that "Gabriel" was not a human person, which we have suggested angels are. No man could live such a long period of time. But in the study of the word "Gabriel" we find that it is translated in the Hebrew "valiant men"(two Hebrew root words, "*gabar*" which means strong, valiant and "*el*" which means mighty). It is the same word that David used calling his better soldiers "valiant men" (1 Chronicles 7:2).

So the word "Gabriel" is not a name as we suppose because of the way that it is translated by the KJV but rather is simply a word that means "valiant men." Now, why would the word "Gabriel" be used in the Old Testament and the New Testament? The angel is one with a divine message, a valiant man, a servant of God bringing forth the word of God from out of the heavens.

Angels are Men

Again it bears repeating that Revelation 21:17 KJV states: "*...according to the measure of a man, that is of the angel.*" Moffat reads: "*...by human, that is, by angelic reckoning.*" Young's reads: "*...the measure of a man, that *is, the messenger."* The Greek "angelos" can be translated as angel, messenger. In fact, we find that in the book of Revelation that the angel that gives the word to John tells John not to worship him because he is his brother which obviously would have to be a man. While we cannot discuss every Scripture, good research by the individual will reveal that each angel is a person in the Scripture.

Revelation 22:9 states: "Then he said to me, "See that you do not do that. For I am your **_fellow servant_**." Verse eight states that John was trying to worship an **_angel_**. The actual word servant means "co-slave" in the Greek. This implies that the beings involved together are the same - humans, mankind. The Greek states that it can mean human or divine. But found in common usage in the ancient times it means a person who is a servant or slave.

So who was this "fellow servant," this angel ? We do not know although some suggest it was someone that John recognized and knew. Some people believe that this "angel," this man, was none other than the resurrected Paul. Only conjecture.

Acts 7:53 reads: "*who have **_received the law by the direction of angels_** and have not kept it.*" Note that the nation of Israel had received the law from angels. But who were the angels ? The people received the law from Moses and the prophets. Yet, this verse states these men were angels. Were they ? Of course, for the word angel means divine messenger, one sent on a mission to establish the good news. The word "angel" comes from evangel, good news, which is also similar to the word apostle.

The law was from Moses and the prophets (Luke 2:22, John 1:17, James 5:10). These men and women were called of God with a divine message for the hour that had to be proclaimed. Yet, like Gabriel, they were men. The key here is that the Scriptures relate angels synonomously with men.

Galatians 4:14, an inspired verse of scripture, declares the following: "... *but you received me as an **angel of God**, even as Christ Jesus*." While the word "as" implies a similitude, if the word "as" was left out it could still be appropriate. Paul is intimating that his ministry had a divine call, an angelic call which is supported in Galatians 1:1.

These are a few of some verses which indicate that people, that is prophets, ministers, can be angels. Perhaps, outside of scriptures you remember the story of the old man in the store who wished the Lord would visit him. He waited all day and was quite despondent at the Lord not coming. Then the Lord told him that he came into the store as three different people. The moral of the story is that we entertain angels unaware. Scripture seems to support this concept extensively.

Billy Graham, a beloved national evangelist of this century, wrote a book entitled **Angels: God's Secret Agents** in 1975. In one broad brush the book states that angels are "invisible things made by God." He quotes Colossians 1:16 to support his statement (" ...*by Him all things were created that are in heaven and that are on the earth, visible and invisible*). While God does have invisible things created, this verse neither supports nor condemns Graham's position.

Graham goes on to say : "The Bible frequently makes it clear that angels are non-material; Hebrews 1:14 calls them ministering 'spirits'. Intrinsically, they do not possess physical bodies, although they may take on physical bodies when God appoints them to special tasks." The thought presented by Graham suggests that angels are disembodied spirits. The truth is that the Bible states, clearly, categorically and convincingly that only demons are disembodied spirits (Matthew 12:43).

Graham then goes on to say that angels are "sexless" basing his statement on Matthew 22:30 which states: "*Ye do err, not knowing the scriptures, nor the power of God. For in the resurrection they neither marry nor are given in marriage, but are as the angels of God in heaven.*" The only perfect marriage was Adam and Eve. But for the other marriages before the flood it is said there was much "marrying and giving in marriage." We know that Jesus retained his gender after the resurrection for Thomas was told to place his hand in the Lord's hand which had nail scarred holes. Jesus retained His gender as a male, but was sexless, in that he would not allow Himself to produce on a lower plane. Angels are men/women who are in Christ (where there is no male nor female - Galatians 3:28) through the Spirit, but in the natural are totally human. They are angelic because they seek to produce the Christ life in others.

The problem is that the word angel refers to a divine messenger, one given to the ministry of the Lord which has nothing to do with sex. For those who are angels are those given to a divine call.

Scholars agree that the account of the visitors that Abram had in Genesis 18 are the visitation of Father, Son and Holy Spirit. The Spirit of God manifested himself as three angels. Yet, these three were called angels - meaning divine messengers.

The point that we are trying to make is that some previous interpretations by the denominational churches are not accurate when considered in the light of Scripture itself.

A gentleman in the Lord, whom I know, wrote a book on angels which is published through Moody Press. When I raised questions in his Master's Program class concerning some of his interpretations concerning angels we had a discussion about the veracity of some of his tenuous concepts.

Traditional teaching does not necessarily follow the Scriptures. Therefore we shall discuss the following words that are used in consideration of angels: Seraphim, Living Creatures (KJV beasts), Cherubim, Lucifer, Satan.

Chapter Six

SERAPHIM

The word seraphim is plural. The singular is seraph. The singular word, seraph, is used first in Genesis 11:3 where it states that the bricks for the Tower need to be "burned." In Exodus 12:10 the subject of the Passover is discussed and what remains is to be "burned." Both of these and other occurrences suggest a purging of what needs to be removed.

The first occurrence of seraphim is found in Numbers 21:6 where a brass figurine is held up above the people. This figurine is made in the form of a fiery (Hebrew: seraph) serpent (Hebrew: brass, serpent). As you have probably read the account, the people sinned and if they looked on the serpent it would heal them and save their lives.

In Isaiah 6:6 we find that Isaiah feels unclean as he stands before the Lord. The Lord sends the seraphim to him and they cleanse his lips with a hot coal from the altar. Since there was no coal on the altar of incense in the Tabernacle's Holy Place, this spiritually refers to the brazen altar located in the Outer Court, where a sacrifice was slain, representing Christ.

The cleansing which was a burning is to remove the Adamic nature, that sin nature that we inherited from the beginning. Note that the coals were placed on his lips. The type and shadow here is that Isaiah would no longer proclaim things after the flesh but rather after the Spirit of the living God. From this point on Isaiah is no longer identified with the Adamic fallen nature and neither are we when we accept the word brought to us by an angelic messenger who causes us to repent of our sins!

Isaiah is cleansed. We note in Isaiah 6:2 that these creatures had wings, six wings. Two wings covered the face, for no man is known henceforth after the flesh (2 Corinthians 5:16-17) once he has been cleansed. Secondly, the feet are covered for love covers (1 John 2:2) so that we can walk in the path of life and the way of righteousness. Thirdly, the two wings fly which after we have been cleansed, allow us to soar into our heavenly nature having formerly borne the image of the earthly (1 Corinthians 15:49).

Our God is a consuming fire (Hebrews 12:29, Deuteronomy 4:24). Thus, the seraphim are an extension of His very own nature. Since we must be holy as He is holy, the seraphim ministry is always focused on the Adamic nature to remove it, purge it from our new mind in Christ Jesus. That is why it states that they are around the throne of God in 6:2. (A corollary to this is our cassette tape and a written message on Uzziah).

The ministry of the seraphim extends to even Sheol (Psalm 139:8). For judgment is given into their hands. Just as Isaiah was judged by these angels, realize that these angels were not some winged creature in the natural but a human being performing the work of God in the life of the individual.

The Lake of Fire, an Angelic Ministry

The furnace of affliction is found in this life, it is called the lake of fire. As one reads in Revelation 19:20, and 20:14-15 we can find some things that relate to the Isaiah 6 verses. Before we discuss that we need to note that Hebrews 1:7 reiterates Psalm 104:4. Careful study will show that **men** are the ministers of fire. These same men then are angels (and we know that the word angel means a messenger of God with good news). These men are the reapers of the Lord (Matthew 13:39). They gather and burn the chaff in the same season as the harvesting of the wheat, which is threshed on the winnowing floor.

We find then in Revelation 19:20 the beast and false prophet were cast into the lake of fire. While it may seem farfetched, nevertheless, we will use the words in the Scriptures to explain themselves. A "lake" is a body of water. Since this book is allegorical, we find the water to represent the Spirit throughout the Bible. The lake is a body of water. The key here is body. The corporate expression of the life of God is the church, the body of Christ.

It is also noted that this is a lake of fire, which in the natural is close to impossible. Since it is allegorical, why the fire? The fire is to purify, remove the corruption. Brimstone (Revelation 20:10) also used in the lake of fire is the word for sulphur in English. As a child, my mother would pour yellow sulpha powder into cuts and wounds to heal them. We use sulpha drugs to bring healing today.

Isaiah 66:15 states: "... the Lord will come with fire...flames of fire.... judge all flesh." He has made his ministers a flame of fire (Hebrews 1:7), a seraphim ministry to bring judgment on those who have the mark of the beast. <u>The mark of the beast is not some future event to occur in the literal but rather has occurred since Adam. The mark of the beast is the carnal nature</u> which has sealed all mankind to one fate - the lake of fire, the ministry of purification through the body of Christ, the lake itself.

He was a pillar of fire to the Israelites in the wilderness, guiding them. Jeremiah states that His word shut up in him was a fire (20:39). For His word is life and removes all death, purges it. *"Who among us can dwell with the everlasting burnings? He who walks righteously and speaks uprightly."* (Isaiah 33:14) Fire only hurts those with the mark of the beast nature which is seen in the false prophet and the beast.

The lake of fire is to remove the beast nature, that fallen nature which is at enmity with God. This can be done only through annihilation, total destruction, for the soul that sins dies (Ezekiel 18:4) except by the grace of God. Psalm 50:3 states that a lake of fire is around His throne. See also Psalm 97:3. No corruption can stand before God's presence.

It is the ministry of the seraphim that delivers creation from the bondage of corruption. We read in 2 Peter 3:9-10 the following: "*...not willing that any should perish but that all should come to repentance. But the day of the Lord will come as a thief in the night, in which the heavens shall pass away with a great noise, and the elements will melt with fervent heat; both the earth and the works that are in it will be burned up.*"

In Genesis God destroyed the earth with water - what earth? It is still here. He destroyed Adam, mankind who was made of the earth. He promised never to do it again that way. So now He is destroying the earth again by fire. Not the natural earth, but those who dwell in the earth (Rev.12:12). That is to say those who dwell in the earth nature, that carnal nature. We see the results of this daily where the darkness of man's evil ways are exposed and judged.

The seraphim ministry is an Outer Court and Holy Place ministry. We remember reading in Acts 2 that the Holy Spirit descended as "flames of fire" on the heads of the disciples and others. They spoke with authority and 3,000 were added to the church in one day. Miraculous. Yes, for the flesh of the fallen nature, that Adamic nature, that earth realm nature was removed as if it were scales from blind eyes. The fire of the Lord found in the ministers of God cleansed the sanctuary of the Lord, the mind, of the unsaved. Judgment came to the house of the Lord, His very temple which you are.

The seraphim ministry is to cleanse the household of God, as it did in the wilderness. This fire ministry is to remove the carnal nature right out of the church. However, most have been taught an escapist mentality that they would be perfected after they get to heaven which is an erroneous misapplication of the Scriptures. The fire of Daniel was not to destroy the saint but to reveal the Christ nature during the fire that the King might get saved.

Consequently, fire is good for the saint and the sinner. For the sinner the fire is unto redemption and release from corruption. For the saint the fire is unto perfection and release of Him who is in them. Rejoice then when a minister of fire, a seraph, comes your way.

Chapter Seven

THE CHERUBIM, WHO ARE THEY?

The Cherubim are different from the seraphim. The Cherubim are found in the Holy of Holies. They minister from the Tabernacle's realm in contrast to the seraphim who minister from the realm of Passover (Outer Court) and Pentecost (Holy Place). When God had Israel make the Tabernacle, He told them to fashion the Holy of Holies with Cherubim. It is to this that we turn.

Exodus 25:22 reads: *"And there will I meet with you, and I will speak with you from above the mercy seat from between the two cherubim."* The LORD spoke from the Holy of Holies. He did not speak in the realm of Passover where the brazen altar and the laver were nor did He speak from the Holy Place where the candlestick, showbread and altar of incense were located. He spoke out of the Holy of Holies. All other realms - Passover (salvation) Pentecost (baptism of the Holy Spirit) are established or brought forth out of Tabernacles or the Holy of Holies.

Hebrews 7:16 states that Jesus was after the order of Melchizedec and had the power of an endless life. The realm of the Holy of Holies reveals the life of God and the fullness of it. Lucifer, the anointed Cherub, had the power of an endless life but chose the way of vanity. The two Cherubs (Cherubim is plural, Cherub singular) in the Holy of Holies represent the witness of life, two being the number of witness. It is only as we behold Christ that we become like Him. The Cherubs face each other and it is only as we look through God's eyes (the cloud of smoke or glory which resided between the Cherubim, that we can see the Christ in each person and become Him as we behold Him.

Exodus 25:18 states: *"And you shall make two Cherubim of gold; of hammered work you shall make them at the two ends of the mercy seat."* Gold speaks of divinity. We who now are being released from the bondage of corruption to enter into the image of Christ (Romans 8:20) have an incorruptible seed within (1 Peter 1:23) that is angelic, a divine messenger, that is growing and is fully gold, of His nature. This seed can only produce Him. Note that these Cherubim are of hammered work. There is a formation process of this new creation within that is handcrafted by God. Did you know that gold can be hammered so thin that one can see through it as glass ? Yes, that He who is in us can be seen through.

Exodus 25:19 goes on to say that the Cherubim were of *"...one piece with the mercy seat."* This means that the Cherubim are identified with the full merciful nature of God, having been conformed to His nature. Union with Christ is full identification with Him and the recognition that Adam does not exist when you are residing in Him. Such identification (Romans 8:1) creates a liberty to flow in the presence of God.

Chapter 26:1 of Exodus states: *"Moreover you shall make the Tabernacle with ten curtains woven of fine linen thread, and blue and purple and scarlet yarn; with artistic designs of Cherubim shall you weave them."* The Tabernacle consisted only of two realms - Pentecost and Tabernacles. The Passover, the outer court was not part of the Tabernacle. The Tabernacle represents the Holy of Holies (Spirit) and the Holy Place (mind/soul). The Tabernacle was made of curtains that had Cherubim woven into them.

Ten in the scriptures represents personal testing. Blue represents heavenly things. Purple represents royalty. Scarlet reveals the blood of Christ. Taking these into account, the Cherubim reflect the heavenly realm, unending life, the fullness of God which Lucifer, Adam, was before he fell.

These Cherubim that were interwoven with the curtains are spiritually interpreted. The soul is to be married to the Spirit, even as Heaven and Earth are one - neither can exist without the other. This is the spiritual house eternal in the heavens made for us without hands (2 Corinthians 5).

Revelation 4:6 states that the beasts which correspond 100% with Ezekiel chapter 1 are "living." The word "living" in the Greek means "self-existent." That is, the life in them which was God Himself was so pervasive that their life was hid in God through Christ. These Cherubim had entered into the realm of life that has no beginning nor end. They had moved from the realm of Adam, who had a beginning and because of sin an ending, and were now alive in Christ.

One of the discussions that I had with the man teaching the Master's Program at Moody was that the Cherubim and the Living Creatures (KJV beasts) were one in the same. His premise was that these were two different "types" or "classes" of angels. But we find the following information in the Bible in Ezekiel 10:20 which states: *"This is the living creature....and I knew they were the Cherubim."* The word creature is singular here and Cherubim is plural, but there is no difficulty with that since the living creature had four manifestations, the same as the Cherubim in Revelation 4. But they are not separate "classes"; rather they are one in the same as Ezekiel declares.

The Four Faces of the Cherubim are Man's Personality Groups.

The Gospels reveal the four faces of Christ (lion, man, ox, eagle) which correspond to the basic four personality types found in psychological studies. Yet, these four are also related to the four faces of the Cherubim in Ezekiel and Revelation. The Cherubim are nothing more than men!

As one studies the Scriptures, the four faces of Christ in the Gospels stand out in many ways. Natural man has discerned that there are four basic personality types in the world (some subdivide them even further). This truth, like all truth, comes from God. All throughout Scripture four is the number of witness in the world. The Gospels reveal the four different "faces" of Christ. Each face does correspond to a personality type.

In a marriage, each personality is God-given and must be recognized as such. This is a difficult problem for two specific reasons. First, we each have a tendency to move in the syndrome that the spouse should conform to the way we think and do things. This is epidemic in marriages! When a spouse sees his/her partner from this syndrome, the spouse is viewing the person either from the Adamic, fallen nature OR from his/her own personality, which has its own way of viewing things. Your personality is God-given and the way it views things is correct for it, but it will not agree with a person with one of the other three personality types. It takes all four jointly to give a true picture. Thus, we have four Gospels in the Scriptures. Each reveals a facet of the Lord Jesus' personality. How do the Gospels do it? Each writer looks from his perspective, his own personality.

As one studies the Cherubim we find that Ezekiel 1 and 2 show that the living creatures also have four faces that correspond to the faces of the flags or banners of the leading Israelite tribes. In Numbers 2:3 we find that Issachar and Zebulun rally around the flag of the tribe of Judah. Genesis 49:8-10 reveals that the **Lion** is the symbol of the tribe of Judah as well as a face of the living creatures in Ezekiel. Judah was placed at the East side of the camp before the Tabernacle entrance. The Lion is also a symbol of kingship and the Gospel of Matthew reveals Jesus as the King ruling in the kingdom of God. On the South side is the tribe of Reuben whose flag sways with the symbol of a **Man**, also a face of the Cherubim. On the West side of the camp is the flag of Ephraim which like the Cherubim has a symbol of the **Ox**. On the North side of the Tabernacle is the tribe of Dan (Numbers 2) whose symbol is that of an **Eagle**. The Eagle corresponds to the face of the Cherubim and also to the Gospel of John which constantly shows Jesus as the overcomer, the conqueror.

Matthew - the Lion

One would have to study the Gospels a little to see some major differences between them, but if an in depth study is done, the peculiarities of each are pronounced and reveal so much of our Lord. Matthew reveals our Lord as a LION, as a KING, and the use of the word "kingdom" is quite prevalent in his writings. In fact, the opening verse declares "the book of generations of Jesus Christ." Matthew establishes immediately the genealogy of Christ as well as His heritage of kingly rights. Here Jesus is traced to Abraham to show His lineage is of the "promised seed." In contrast, Luke traces Jesus' lineage to Adam, revealing Jesus as a man descended from Adam. Both are valid but each reveals a different facet of the Lord.

Again going a little further, Jesus' birth in Matthew is connected with the genealogy of His Kingship and with the thought that Jesus is <u>descending</u> from heaven; whereas Luke connects His birth with His baptism and His humanity and His <u>ascending</u> from that to His Lordship and manifestation as the Son at the baptism. In fact, to my knowledge, no writer of the Gospels other than Matthew states that a "governor" (Matthew 2:6) comes out of Israel. This too reveals quite simply that Matthew sees the Lord from the perspective as a dominant, authoritative, take charge, leader-type of person. This view reveals Christ as a Choleric personality type.

The dominant (choleric) personality is very much like a king. For this person envisions the correct way to do things, and when asked to make a decision is generally 90% correct. While there is a tendency to make such a decision from a fleshly point of view, if in the Spirit, this leader will listen to counsel and make good decisions. This person is progressive in his ideas, and his value is his ability to confront issues (sometimes without concern for the other person's feelings). This personality type has a tendency to view others by his performance, rather than their relationship. Yet, this personality type will work within the system, although he will remain somewhat of a loner. Within a team concept this person would feel a little more comfortable by doing his own job that is part of the team goal rather than working with others as a group to accomplish the goal together.

Mark - the Ox

On the West side of the camp was the leading banner of Ephraim, which means "double fruitfulness." The symbol for this tribe also coordinates with the Gospel of Mark. For here we see a man who is in the ministry and active in the "doing" of the work. As one reads Mark we notice that Mark refers to the "service" of the Lord. Mark calls the gospel the "gospel of the Son." Here he means that Jesus came to serve. In Mark we read, "He ordained the twelve that they might be with Him." This also reveals the thought that Jesus wanted these twelve to share with Him in ministry, i.e. service.

Perhaps a small contrast with Matthew would be helpful. At the Last Supper, Matthew records: *"They began to say, Lord, is it I?"* But Mark records: *"They began to say unto Him, one by one, Is it I?"* He omits the word "Lord." This is true in quite a few instances between Matthew and Mark. Matthew is always looking at things from a governmental point of view (Kingdom). But Mark looks at it from an identification with Jesus with the thought of ministry or service. Another feature of Mark is his showing of tenderness, of which a service-oriented person will consider. Examine the following Scriptures in Mark and then compare them with the other Gospels and you will see the difference. Speaking of the little children Mark states: "...took them up in his arms." Or of Peter's mother he states: *"took her by the hand and lifted her up."* Only in Mark do we find the line *"Jesus, looking upon him..."* when talking to the man seeking eternal life.

Thus, the servant personality is apparent. This person will correspond with the Phlegmatic personality type. Willing to work at a task, faithful, hard working, detail oriented etc. Jesus reveals this in Mark and is a good study for this personality type because the revelation of Jesus here in Mark fits that personality type. We see concern, loving outreach, understanding, a willing ear to listen which are all admirable traits. Perhaps the most interesting statement used frequently by the book of Mark is the word "compassion." It is used here more than in any other book of the Bible. This personality type is truly a compassionate person.

Luke - the Man

On the South side of the camp the rallying tribe was that of Reuben found in Numbers 2:10. Reuben was the first born who lost his birthright to Judah because of his incestuous sin. Yet, he was not cut off and was still the leader in the family because of birthright. Reuben's symbol was that of a man, for Luke shows Jesus as a man.

In contrast to Matthew which lists the genealogy of Jesus based upon His legal right as a ruler and calls Him the Son of God, Luke lists Jesus' lineage as that of the Son of Man. Luke writes revealing the Melancholy personality type using this facet of Jesus' nature so that those born with that nature might have great encouragement. It is in Luke that we read the words that Joseph and Mary "went up to be taxed." Again Luke shows Jesus as the one who has descended and identified with us; whereas, Matthew shows the wise men coming and giving offerings unto the King of Kings. Incredible the difference of focus of each personality isn't it? Yet, each is valid and true. We need not think someone who is different is wrong or carnal etc. because they do not think like us nor act like we do. Again Luke deals with the natural man in that Jesus was offered before the priest on the eighth day for circumcision. None of the others mention this nor do they say that He was 30 when His ministry began. Luke focuses on the man. The word "prayer" is used more in Luke than in all the other gospels. Here again a man would have a need for prayer far more than God. And that is the point of Luke's writing about the Lord. He wanted to show

Jesus as a man and His struggles as a man. This would help the Melancholy person who is given over at times to despondency or even rage. At the same time, this personality type is given to details and quality control and is very concerned about the little things that make a difference, and Luke reveals these important details of Jesus.

John - the Eagle

The Gospel of John reveals Christ as an eagle, the overcomer. This Gospel constantly, more so than all the others, speaks of and uses the word "life" voluminously. We see this personality as the vivacious one, the enthusiastic person who is Sanguine in nature. In this gospel we see Jesus revealed as the one who knows everyone. John is known as the disciple Jesus loved. John is "center stage" as he is the one leaning on Jesus' breast. Jesus' emotions are illustrated at the last supper, with Mary and Martha, Lazarus' tomb, and after His resurrection when He appears by the sea teaching Peter about love. In chapter 5-7 Jesus is contrasted with the law (the tendency of Luke) and walking in grace in that He is shown as fulfilling the law by living in life.

Jesus is seen as the One in which the devil can find nothing (John 14:30) and as the One who has victory over all circumstances (14:33). The Sanguine personality is totally optimistic. Given a lemon, they rejoice and make lemonade. Thus, this face of the Cherubim and the North side of the Tabernacle banner, the eagle, is the epitome of life. I am sure you have met people who are "the life of the party" with their cheerful attitude (Jesus said be of good cheer 16:33). Such is this type of person.

Each person has resident in them all four types of personality but one "colors" or predominates the others. The Gospels reveal each facet of each one and in that sense reveal the very fullness of Jesus to us. As we study marriage/union with God, we must be aware that each personality is given of God and is good. We must discern the "Christ" in the other. May it enhance the revelation of our Lord Christ Jesus in you and in others.

Lucifer : Satan OR Adam ?

But that only leads us to Ezekiel 28:14 which states: "You were the anointed Cherub who covers..." Isaiah 14 is one of two chapters that is used to teach the religious concept that Satan is Lucifer. Careful reading will show that the prophecy is given to the nation of Israel about its return from Babylon (verses 3,4) which had not yet occurred. Secondly, it states in verse 16 that this is a **man**. It is not a spirit. Verse 16 reads: "*Is this **the man** that made earth to tremble.*" In fact, we know that it refers to the Babylonian king but also we know that it is specifically referring to a man because in 14:11 it states: "...*down to the **grave**...*" and Satan, an evil spirit, is not involved going to the grave. Grave is used for people, humans and not for spirits. The word used for grave is the Hebrew word "sheol" which has been used continuously for "hell" in the KJV. Note also the use of the word "worm" in verse 11. Worms help work on rotting bodies and Satan is a spirit without a body. We can also see from verse 19 that the word "slain" and "carcass" is used. Nowhere in Scripture does it state that Satan is slain.

There is another concern that has to be addressed. We note that Lucifer has fallen (14:12). The teachers that relate this to Satan have erred in their understanding Scriptures because John 8:44 states otherwise: "*You are of your Father the devil....He was a **murderer from the beginning**.*" Satan never fell. He was a murderer from the beginning, from the very start of creation. Whereas, we see that Lucifer fell. Who then is Lucifer ? It cannot be Satan. Whereas, in Isaiah 14:13-14 we note that Lucifer states: "...*I will ascend into the heavens. I will exalt my throne above the stars of God... I will be like the Most High.*" Satan was evil from the beginning. <u>He could not exalt himself nor could he be cast down because he was evil from the</u> beginning.

Romans 8:20 states: " *For the creature was subject to vanity, not willingly but by reason of Him who has subjected the same in hope.*" The "creature" here refers to Adam. The weakness in Adam was exploited by the serpent. Who was the serpent ? Revelation 12:9 states the serpent is Satan. It was Adam who tried to ascend and be like God, via the deception of Satan. Thus, we see that Adam fell from his lofty position in God.

Does this make sense ? Yes, it does because Luke 3:38 states that Adam was a son of God. Adam had the power to become a son of God (John 1:8) as you do also (Romans 8:19). But Adam accepted less than what was offered.

In reading 2 Peter 1:19 we find that Jesus is referred to as the "Day Star" who is to arise in our hearts. We note in Isaiah 14:2 that Lucifer, the Light Bearer, was the son of the morning, which is what the Day Star is called. We who have been called to walk in the image, be conformed to the image of Christ are to have the Day Star arise in us. In other words, we are in one sense to return to what Adam could have had before the fall.

There is **_no_** verse in the Bible that states that Lucifer is a name for Satan. Satan is called other names but nowhere does it refer to Satan as Lucifer. The actual word translated "Lucifer" is used only once in the Hebrew in the Old Testament. It should be translated "light bearer" or "brightness". Jesus has said of us, that we are to be the "light of the world." Adam was the "light" in his day. Adam was to set the pattern for us. We must remember that Satan **masquerades** as an angel of light, but is only full of darkness (2 Corinthians 11:14)! So, Satan could not be Lucifer. Consequently, the Day Star that arises in our hearts is Christ Jesus, and since we are to be in His image it is logical that Lucifer was called son of the morning in Isaiah 14. As we read Daniel 12:3 it states: *"Those who are wise shall shine like the brightness of the firmament."* This refers to those who are conformed to the One who is Wisdom, Christ Jesus. Hopefully, the reader will see the relationship between this verse and Isaiah 14:12.

Now, if Adam was a son of God as Luke 3:38 states, then we need to see what he really looked like before the fall as a "light bearer." The next Scripture we need to look at is in Ezekiel 28. Here in verse 12 it states: *"Son of man take up a lamentation upon the king of Tyre and say unto him, 'Thus, saith the Lord God, thou sealest up the sun, full of wisdom and perfect beauty. Thou hast been **in Eden the garden of God**, every precious stone was thy covering, the sardis, topaz, diamond, beryl, onyx, jasper, sapphire, emerald and the carbuncle, and gold the workmanship of thy timbrels and pipes was prepared in thee in the day that thou was created.'"*

Was Jesus full of wisdom? Luke 2:52 states that Jesus grew in the wisdom and stature of the Lord. Thus, Ezekiel 28:12 could relate to Adam before the fall, in the stature of Christ (Ephesians 4:12-13). In Psalms, David sought the beauty of the Lord (27:4). But we find Hebrews 1:3 states: "...Who being the brightness of His glory and the express image of His person." This refers to Christ Jesus.

Ezekiel refers to Adam who was made in the image of God (Genesis 1:27).

<u>The key here is that of all mankind only can it be said of Adam that he</u> <u>was in the garden of Eden</u>. Adam was perfect in the way that he was created. Adam fell because he thought he was the source of his own power, but Satan was evil from the beginning. It was the suggestion planted by the serpent, Satan, that caused Adam to fall.

But to make sure that we understand that Lucifer is Adam, we need to read carefully Isaiah 14:16 which states: "...*is this the man*" or Ezekiel 28:15 which states: "..*till iniquity was found in you*..." which refers also to Romans 8:20. Iniquity was found in man, not in Satan.

Perhaps with some careful study the reader will determine that Lucifer is Adam and not Satan as tradition teaches.

Chapter Eight

THE BEASTLY IMAGE

We have heard much preaching on the image of the beast. The worry, fear and anxiety caused by the concern for the mark of the beast is totally unfounded. God, our loving Father, does not cause fear, worry or anxiety. Rather He loves us so that He has promised many times that He will never desert us. In fact, perfect love casts out fear (1 John 4:18). Those who are Christians do not walk in fear for such a mark is not on them.

We should have no concern for a certain man appearing as the antichrist. We should have no concern for the stamp 666. These are but carnal interpretations of the Word of God. After all, it is not what is on the outside of man that declares his nature but rather what comes out of him (Matt. 15:17-20). We fight not against earthly institutions and governments. Rather our fight is with principalities and powers of the air (Ephesians 6:12). These are not natural powers we fight against, but wickedness and corruption in high places. What are the high places? The high places are the minds of men. It is a spiritual warfare.

The beastly image is our concern. This image can be readily seen abounding in mankind. <u>You do not have to look for the mark of the beast - you have inherited it from the fallen nature of Adam</u>. The good news is that there are only two men in the world - Adam and Christ. One of them is dead and the other is alive. Your life is hid in the one alive. The carnal mind employs the use of the beastly nature. The beastly nature can be seen in fleshly manifestations of lusts of all sorts. Whether these be fulfilled by bodily action or mental thought, they are the beastly nature. The mark of the beast is not a literal stamp in the forehead or in the hand but truly is the fallen nature of the person! There is no need to look for a mark - one can see it all over the world on many people. The mark that the lusts leave is the beastly image. Those of the same nature can not discern such carnality, but those who have the mind of Christ can see it plainly.

Revelation 13:14 states that only those who dwell in the earth can be deceived. This is not the natural earth, but rather describes the person who dwells in the nature of Adam, that fallen nature, which was made of the earth (Genesis 2:7). As one reads on in chapter 13 he comes to verse 16 which states: *"to receive the mark on their right hand OR on their forehead."* Note that both do not occur. These are not literal marks, for the beastly nature is already active in the world. The mark in the hand is symbolic of the one who "does" the work of the beast, evil things.

Leviticus 14 declares that the priest (a type of Christ) anoints the hand with oil, after it has been cleansed by the blood, which speaks of salvation. This anointing speaks of the Holy Spirit baptism. In direct contrast, the fallen nature, that beastly nature, is covered by the blood of slain Abel and is anointed by the carnal mind. So, the hand that is put to the work of the flesh carries it out.

Yet, Leviticus 14 continues, an immeasurable amount of oil is placed on the head of the saint to be cleansed, the third step of the process. This speaks of Tabernacles, and union with God. He who is joined to the Lord is one spirit, scripture declares. In contrast, IF the beastly person is not anointed for cleaning as in Leviticus 14, a mark is already given, even as Cain had a mark on him (Genesis 4:15). A sealing, if you will, that signifies the individual is a prisoner of the carnal mind and thoughts thereof.

It is important to note that the mark is on their hand **or** their forehead. It is not in both places. Typical teachings in this day age depict both in that person. This presents fear to the Christian, and the unsaved are totally unaware that they have the mark already working in them. Strange isn't it? The ones who should repent and seek God are unaware. The ones saved are scared and fearful worrying about their life. The answer to that later.

Most Christians have not read Revelation 7:3. It has not been preached to them. Let me quote it: "***Do not harm the earth, the sea, or the trees <u>until we have sealed the servants of our God</u> in their foreheads***." There is no destruction done to the saint. He who has his life hid in God, though he would burn at the stake, feels nothing. **<u>Foxe's Book of Martyrs</u>** reveals that many saints killed for the witness they had, sang as they burned at the cross. How so? Their life was hid in God and that life is above the natural life and empowers the saint. The Old Testament priest had a gold nameplate across the mitre. It signified that his mind was sealed, holy to God. We have the mind of Christ. Some may be more immature in it, but every Christian is in Christ and a new creature, no longer known after the flesh, after Adam (2 Corinthians 5:16).

In accepting the deception of Satan in the garden, Adam and Eve thought they were being spiritual and seeking spiritual things. They accepted the fruit in order to be like gods. Yet, what they thought was a spiritual move and a good wholesome endeavor was nothing more than total carnality. Before the fall they were already in the image of the Father. However, that beastly image was emerging from the depths of their being masquerading as truth when in reality it was death, deception and a lie (2 Corinthians 11:14).

The beastly image will always manifest itself, and at every opportunity it will try to satisfy its corrupt nature. I once knew a man who knew I was an insurance agent and came to my door to buy insurance. He said the Lord told him to buy the policy. He kept it a few months and dropped it. I asked him why and he replied that the Lord had told him to do it. There was not an extenuating financial crisis in his life to cause him to drop the insurance. But his carnal mind was quite active, even as a Chrsitian. How carnal that man was. If God had told him to take the policy in the first place, God, Who is changeless, would not have told him to drop it. Rather it was the man's flesh, that beastly nature, that appeared as God speaking to him. If allowed to, that beastly image within the breast of man will destroy the man of God.

The carnal man is concerned about a physical mark on his body, which he thinks is the mark of the beast. <u>But in reality, his own carnality is the mark of the beast that he so fears</u>. Paul declared that he bore the marks of Christ in his body (Galatians 6:17). Of course in the natural there were many marks on his body from the whippings, floggings and the many hardships he faced. But beloved, there was also another marking that could be found, and that mark was the image of Christ. In Galatians he declared that henceforth no man could trouble him any longer in the flesh. Why? Because he bore the image of Christ, and the carnal man couldn't touch him. It no longer had a part of him. John in 1 John 5:18 states: "***We know that whoever is born of God does not sin; but he who has been born of <u>God keeps himself, and the wicked one does not touch him</u>***." He who is in Christ cannot be touched by Satan. The Christian who has not matured can be touched because the youthful saint has trouble believing that he is in Christ and he focuses on his old nature rather than God the finisher of his faith.

It is important to note that what John wrote is verified by Christ Himself in John 14:30 where Jesus states: *"... for the ruler of this world is coming, and he has nothing in me."* There was no darkness in Jesus and there is no darkness in a saint, although many churches teach that there is. One reason for teaching that the saint is still a sinner but saved by grace is so that the believer is held in a place of bondage to the church system.

Consider both the image of the beast and the image of Christ. Which do you bear in your body? The beastly image is very religious at times. It has an air of outward holiness about it. Many Christians bear the religious beastly mark. Some consider certain types of clothing, hair, etc. to be the prerequisite for holiness. Others are caught up in church rituals and traditions, which are regarded as truth. The use and pleasure of these things by the religious beastly image is nothing more than hidden pride. This image denies that holiness is right standing with God and not solely based on outward appearances. Our righteousness is not based on the doing of things or religiosity but on the grace of God.

The beastly image preaches a gospel of regulation and legislates holiness to the saints. Worship must be on certain days, the Ten Commandments must be kept, and all works are done to receive a reward from heaven. Such vanity denies that we live by grace and emphasizes works. Christians under this bondage feel condemned if they do not attend every church function. If we truly live by the grace of God, in the inChristed image, we have no condemnation.

The beastly nature is found in sinful man. Those in Christ, although living in a physical body, do not have to conform to the sin nature. They may dwell in an earthen body, but their residence is found in Christ. Paul truly declared, *"It is no longer I that liveth, but Christ that liveth in me."* (Gal.2:20)

Perhaps it should be noted that many who have the baptism of the Holy Spirit are controlled by the carnality of the beastly image. Paul declared that the Corinthian church was in such a state. Their beastly desires overruled their spiritual gifts. Many of their spiritual gifts were used for personal profit and gain - a true sign of the control of the beastly nature.

The greatest deception is the subtleness of the enemy. Many have heard the voice of God say that death to the self-nature is required. Most believers after some study of the Scriptures know that they must put on Christ and cast the old nature away. Yet, the beastly image appears when they think they can help themselves die to the old nature. There is a failure to grasp the idea of putting on the Lord Jesus Christ. This literally means "sink into" Him in the Greek. See references in Ephesians 4:24 and Galatians 3:27.

Have you ever let yourself go and fallen into bed? If you have experienced that then you know there is no struggle nor fear of missing the bed. You just totally relax and let go, and the soft bed envelopes you. This is what "sink into" means, i.e. "putting on" Christ. The King James Version implies striving and struggling to put on something, like clothes, etc. Struggling is a beastly way. We walk by grace. We just need to rest and sink into the flow of the Spirit, and God will direct our paths. He will do it because of His good pleasure.

<u>The beastly image is not a physical mark but rather a lifestyle</u>. An unbeliever lives his life totally controlled by the fallen beastly nature. A Christian is delivered from that

nature by the work of the cross. He can fall back into the lie of the beastly image if he is not careful. (Gal.4:9-11).

Before God made the individual man in His image, He had a concept of the corporate man, in His image. The individual was to be a part of the whole. Consequently, when we see the beastly image, that man of sin, we see a corporate expression of him too. The first man created was Adam, which means mankind, and was made of the earth. To the earth he shall return - corporately and individually. 1 Corinthians 15 clearly shows that the old nature cannot inherit the life that God has for us.

Now then, the resurrection of Jesus was individual but it also was corporate in that He who was raised from the dead raised all the new creations with Him (Eph 4:24, Romans 6:4). He was raised as a corporate expression and we were in Him, yea, even from the foundation of the world.

The salvation of the world was destined from the beginning and it is to be accomplished through a people, a corporate expression who will do greater things than He did (John 14:12).

This corporate expression is in direct opposition to the concentrated image that the Christian religious world focuses on. The church system has taught people to look upon the decimation, the devastation and destruction that is coming, when in reality they should be concentrating on developing the Christ life in their vessels. Everywhere the church is trying to decide what is the mark of the beast, when they should be focusing on the sealing of Christ. The people have been blinded by the teachings of false leaders who do not prepare them to be the manifestation of Christ in the earth.

There can be no doubt that the world is filled with the beastly image, but it is a passing order as the saints identify with their God and do not fear nor see this false identity. Secondly, the beastly image is not an external thing that will be seen, but rather is the manifestation of the internal carnal nature. <u>As long as saints externalize their faith, it is not a real faith, but is a faith of the carnal man, that beastly image</u>.

Chapter Nine

THE APOSTASY

"Don't let anyone deceive you in any way, for that day will not come until the rebellion occurs and the man of lawlessness is revealed, the son of perdition." (NIV)
2 Thessalonians 2:3

Only one time in the Holy Scriptures does the word "apostasy" occur. In the King James Version of the Bible it is translated as "falling away." Yet, this one-time usage is the foundation of many a theological thought. The Greek word which is transliterated as apostasy means: "defection from the truth, being separated from truth, to be removed and desist from truth."

Truth is not a "thing". Truth is not an object or physical creation on the earth. Truth is not knowledge or wisdom, although both may have truth in them. Truth is not a "what". Nor can it be a "when". We can not say "where" a truth is. Truth is none of the above. By seeking after truth most people look to understand something. But that is not truth either.

Truth is a Person. Truth is Jesus Christ (John 14:6). He is the very express image of the Father (Hebrews 1:1). All that He is reveals the very nature of truth. When He speaks, He speaks out of truth. When He walks, He reveals the truth about walking and how it is perfectly done. All that He says, does, and thinks is done in truth. Thus, He is truth. His actions are based upon the very nature of Himself, which is the nature of God, and therefore He cannot act outside of His nature which is pure, unadulterated, holy truth.

Developing a relationship with Christ Jesus will, by the Holy Spirit, lead you into all truth (John 16:13). In other words the Holy Spirit will lead you into Him who is truth and you will become Him because of the change that comes from entering a relationship with Christ. Spiritual growth is Jesus Christ. It is His life, His very creative powers that will lead us into the maturity of Christ (Ephesians 4:12-16). Christ is the very opposite of apostasy. Apostasy is at the other end of the spectrum, even as light is far removed from darkness.

"Defection from truth" is one of the definitions of the word apostasy. I think that it may easily be stated in another way: "Apostasy is defection from Jesus Christ." Since Jesus Christ is truth, defection from truth is a one-hundred and eighty degree change in direction. Apostasy therefore happens when one had a relationship that was begun with Christ but over time this relationship turned against Him. It is a defection from an intimate closeness with God.

One cannot be part of an apostasy or falling away UNLESS one has had a relationship with Jesus Christ. The apostasy occurs among CHRISTIANS. It does not occur among the unregenerated or the unsaved. <u>The pagan who has never been acquainted with Christ through a personal experience is NOT an apostate. You cannot fall away from something that you have never experienced. Apostate religion is that which has fallen away from Christ Jesus</u>.

The key is trying to define what is considered "falling away." It is not easily discerned "who" has fallen away. What one saint considers a defection from God another considers moving on with God. As a Baptist I was taught "speaking in tongues" was a thing from the devil. But when I received this gift from my Father, I realized I was wrong to call something from Him as a thing of the devil! Many times defection from the truth is determined from which side of the fence one is looking. In reality, I, the Baptist, was defecting from the truth.

The "falling away" comes from saints who have left the truth. Truly, it is in God's hands as to whether they have left or paused in their relationship with Him. But the point to be considered is that the saint who falls away is worse off than the person who never knew God. Many times in Scripture the phrase OUTER DARKNESS is used, it is used in relation with a servant of the Lord (Matthew 25:30) or the children of the kingdom (Matthew 8:12). Darkness is where the unbeliever is found. But OUTER DARKNESS is reserved for the saint who has fallen by the wayside.

Yet, typical teaching is that the "falling away" is tied to the last portion of the of 2 Thessalonoians 2:3 which is: *"the man of sin, the son of perdition."* The idea is that there is ONE person who will appear as the man of sin. This one person will draw away the world. In reality the man of sin is not one literal person, but if the man of sin were one person, he would only draw away the saints because he would already have the world under his control. Yet the church teaches he draws away the world. Looking at this historically one can find a fulfillment for the man of sin which can be read in Josephus' writings of the first century. Josephus saw the Roman general sit in the temple on the mercy seat in the Holy of Holies eating pork! This is considered by the historical school of thought as the fulfillment of 2 Thess. 2:3. This would be possible because Paul was supposed to have written this letter about 55 AD and the Roman takeover of Jerusalem was 70 AD (as was told by Jesus in Matthew 24). If this is acceptable, the Roman general did not draw away the world, but rather drew away those who worshipped at the Jewish temple and were of the Jewish faith.

Another viewpoint held that is historical in nature and definitely more spiritual was produced by the men in the Reformation. Vicar of Christ, the title of the Pope of the Roman Catholic church, means IN PLACE OF Christ. Thus, some reformers believed that the Pope sitting on the throne in the church, was a fulfillment of 2 Thessalonians. This thought also has great historical validity. And the Pope did draw away the church from Christ by keeping the Bible out of their hands, using the doctrine of the Nicolaitans, creating indulgences and penance, besides incorporating into the church pagan customs that were "Christianized."

However, the fallacy of the historical school and the futuristic school (which places the man of sin in a temple some time in the near future) is that both schools of thought are dealing with a LITERAL temple and a JEWISH temple. The Christian church received this letter from Paul, not the Jews. The concern of Paul was with the church and NOT the world. He was NOT concerned with the non-believing Jews and their temple. In fact, Paul uses the word "naos" for temple in this letter. The word for a physical building as a temple or church was "heiron", a totally different word with a totally different meaning. For "naos" is used in 2 Thessalonians 2:4 and also in 1 Corinthians 3:16. Both places refer to the saints' own BODY as the temple. This is far different from a physical building.

Yet, standard theology has misguided the brethren into thinking of a literal man sitting in the seat of a rebuilt temple in the city of Jerusalem. Don't hold your breath on that idea. You may die before it occurs. In the mid 1960's there was a word that stones were being quarried in Indiana for the temple. Many of the saints fell for that as they did for the September '88 rapture! There is not going to be a literal rebuilding of the temple in Jerusalem. God always does things in 3's. Solomon's temple was the first. Nehemiah's was the second temple. The third temple was that of Herod. No more temples will be built, but most Christians today think there will be one because they believe the fundamentalist point of view.

In looking for the apostasy, we must first know where to look. Most saints feel that the world is a good sign of the falling away. This teaching also is false, for the falling away as we mentioned comes from the church itself, not the world. BUT we CAN say that the world will become worse in its paganism, as the Christians fall away from the faith. So, if the world seems to be getting worse, rest assured your eyesight is keen but be cognizant of the fact that it is getting worse because the Christians are forsaking their faith.

The "falling away" cannot occur unless it is in conjunction with the "revelation" of the man of sin. This is why the word "AND" is used in the Scripture. The word "revelation" means the "apocalypse" or the appearing, the uncovering, the revealing, or the disclosure. There has to be a disclosure of corruption. As Christ came to renew our minds, so then the man of sin is made of a carnal mind. So, the revelation that is appearing, even now, is that of the fullness of the carnal mind.

The carnality of the church is being fully revealed as many ministers unfortunately lead from their carnal desires. The preaching of a rapture is a carnal escape mechanism that keeps believers from dealing with the reality of Christ developing in you today. Heaven is preached as a place where we have a party with relatives who have passed on. I declare to you that you won't know any of them for they will all be new in Christ, and you will only know them as they are known - after the Lord. All this carnality, all found in the church, is percolating to a boil. The pot soon will be calling the kettle black.

The man of sin in the church is being revealed by the very hand of God. Judgment begins at the house of the Lord (Rev. 11:1-3, Leviticus 23:28-29). God is allowing all the foolishness of doctrine to be revealed for what it is. Be aware of the false ideas that have crept into the body of Christ.

Within the body of Christ, the sons of God will come forth (Romans 8:14-23). Their spirit is hungering after the Lord irrespective of their location. Whether they are in the system or out of it, there is a group moving amongst the brethren. They seem to be sons for they speak with words that seem to indicate they understand, and they act as if they are. By all appearances they are, but be not deceived.

God has allowed the tares (immature mutated wheat) to grow with the wheat until harvest. In the centuries from Christ until the present it has not been time to clean the house of the Lord from the corruption within, but NOW IT IS. There will be no eastern philosophies in the move of God. There will be no homosexuality in the move of God. There will be no liberty which has degenerated into license. So, the first place where the son of perdition is revealed is from the move of God where the sons come forth.

This too is found in Revelation 11:2. Judgment begins at the house of God. This scripture states to leave out the outer court - the place where the sacrifices are made, that salvational realm or the feast of Passover, where people come to know the Lord Jesus as their Savior. Rather judgment begins IN the temple, the Holy Place which speaks of the baptism of the Holy Spirit or the feast of Pentecost, and the Most Holy Place which speaks of the union with God or the feast of Tabernacles. Judgment begins with those who have been given a deeper understanding by the moving of the Spirit of God in them.

Judgment by the hand of God removes all that proclaims itself holy but does not live it. All that say they are sons are not for if they were, it would be self-evident. The heavens quake. All shall be removed that is not of Him in the third heavens. Judgment begins at the altar of the Holy of Holies (Rev.11). God is presently sifting endtime ministries to prove them. That which remains after the stars fall from heaven will be and now is the visible part of the corporate body of the true sons.

The son of perdition is not an individual man. <u>It is a corporate body of unrepentant saints who sit enthroned in their very own carnal desires</u>. They harvest unto themselves people after the same kind, because the flesh has not been crucified. The "falling away" is the revelation of the corporate body of the son of perdition. It is made up of those who are religious, speak truth but use it for their own self-gratification and consumption rather than being consumed by THE truth. So, they use truth (Christ) to further their own means, but do not allow Christ to consume them.

The end of the age will not come until all that is in the house of God that is not of Him is removed. The sons, the true sons, will not be manifest until all the tares are removed from the threshing floor. The husks, that carnal nature, will be gone by way of the wind (the Spirit).

Only then can the dry bones of Ezekiel 37, those bones dead to the ways of the flesh, come forth in newness of life and the flesh of incorruption and be brought together as the corporate body of the Christ. Quickened, they will stand together as one river, but will be the voice of many waters, as they proclaim release to creation from the bondage of corruption!

The falling away must come first before the son of perdition can be revealed. The falling away comes from the brethren in the church. The end-time situation is somewhat similar to the story of Samson. The call of Samson in the Old Testament was a call to glory. The Lord sought Samson to be a judge in Israel and to set the people free as the anointing of the Lord enabled Samson to deliver the Philistines into Samson's and Israel's hands.

Here was a man that was used mightily of God, and in the end of his life killed more than he had in the whole time he was alive. Many equate the story as a success story. But in reality it is a statement of failure. The spirit of Samson was strong and he desired to serve the Lord. But the flesh, that carnal nature, was even stronger because he chose to feed it first.

He knew the call. He knew that God commanded Israel not to marry persons outside of the faith, i.e. the Philistines. Yet, his flesh overcame his spirit. His strength and call were given without repentance - that is to say, God did not cast off Samson and the mission that Samson had. God still used Samson but the path was not direct; it was "around about." Samson could have done much more for the Lord if he had been obedient.

If his spirit had dominated his flesh, he would not have had to die. He wouldn't have had to die because he wouldn't have been blind. He wouldn't have been blind because he would have been obedient. In the end of his life as he was muzzled, chained and harnessed and ground out the grain like an ox at the mill, he learned to overcome his flesh and allow the Spirit to dominate. It was a lesson learned late in life, but one that God honored when Samson called upon Him.

Even today we see that the church has gone a whoring. Now the difference between a whore and prostitute is great. A whore in scripture is like Rahab, the harlot, whose parents were followers of the Moabite gods. They had left the faith of Israel. A prostitute is one who uses his/her body for literal fornication.

The church has become the great harlot; its members are the ones in Revelation who have fallen away. They have their system, methods, and ways, which are not God's system, method or way. The son of perdition is the one who is produced by the harlot.

We see this plainly today as some who say they are sons are really of the harlot and they are sons of perdition. They have been produced from the false premises that some churches and Christians follow. It is not the true faith that is being revealed but that which is false. Before the sons of God can be revealed, the sons of perdition must be seen.

The eyesight of some of the saints may not be the best. The battle of life on the natural plane at times wears down the saint so that he becomes tired. He sees, but his senses are not sharp to discern. Hebrews 5:14 has not fully been developed in the life of the saint.

Tired of daily fighting the system, the weak Christian is even less likely to open his Bible to study, and if he does open it, it is in the evening when the day is done and he is too! Thus, very little sharpness or spiritual insight will come. Ah, that is why David wrote that we should seek Him early in the day.

The son of perdition offers his ideas to a slumbering giant, the church. The idea creeps into the inner ear as Delilah, which means to make feeble or slacken, speaks soft words which allow the anointing to be removed. Shaved, Samson awakens from slumber to find that his trust in what seemed to be right (the flesh always seems to be right, rational, and logical) was totally incorrect.

The church like Samson is caught in a web that will nearly destroy it. The harlot system is a harlot system because of one simple reason. Not because it has a Romish rake nature, nor is it to be blamed on the denominational daughters, or the independent itinerant. The blame, my friend, lies in the religious nature of the carnal man.

Ah, aren't you a God? For the son of perdition seeks to elevate himself. Yet, God called the backslidden, blasphemous priests gods (elohim). It is no great name but rather the very lowest of natures or manifestations. What our Father has called us to is far higher, purer, holier and more righteous than being an "el" or "elohim", which is what the word "god" means in Hebrew.

For if the carnal nature gets hold of what our Father is really trying to produce in us, the carnal nature will ingest it, digest it, and produce the result on a lower plane. Samson, the church man, heard the call of God in his life. He understood it and for a time was spiritual, but like an adolescent struggling to become a man and yet sometimes acting like a child, Samson was unable to overcome his carnal desires.

Instead of waiting for a spiritual marriage where God would come unto Samson and sup with him and produce the nature of God within, Samson was so enamored with the thought he tried to produce by himself. He shared the pearl of great price. He told the secret before it was produced for God's glory. Thus, Samson brought dishonor to God, since the Philistines, who worshipped Dagon, the fish god, were the very antithesis of true faith.

The desire to be like God, if Godly, will produce Israel, which means "like unto God." <u>But before Israel</u>

became Israel, the old carnal nature of Jacob (supplanter, deceiver) must be removed or it will only reveal the son of perdition producing after the flesh, a poor imitation of what God is doing.

The manifestation of this religious nature can easily be seen. It reveals its serpentine head like a hydra. Chop off one and another appears. The very core of the beast must be removed or it continues to seem to come back to life again, even as in the book of Revelation 18:3 where the wound seemed to be healed.

John wrote in his first epistle that the antichrist was among them even in that day (1 John 2:18-19). The understanding of apostasy isn't time oriented nor event oriented but is rather concerned with conditions of the heart and spirit. The apostasy is among brethren and not outsiders, as we have discussed. The apostasy occurs over many doctrines. The falling away begins when some brethren do not believe similarly. Thus splinter groups, those denominational and nondenominational daughters of the harlot church (Rome), are formed without the true knowledge of God.

Even in the day that Jesus lived there were the Essenes, the Sadducees, and the Pharisees. Of course, there were many others also that interpreted the Old Testament in different ways. The splinter groups were many then, and they are many now. How can they divide Christ ? Christ is not divided. Onyl man's understanding of Him is divided.

John writes that if they were of us, they would have continued with us. It is sad to think that doctrine is more valuable to some than the experience of living in Christ. I heard a story of a minister preaching to his congregation. He stated they were all sinners, and dead. One fellow in the back said outloud for all to hear "I am alive in Christ." He lived by experience in Christ.

How does one deny that Jesus is the Christ? "He is antichrist who denies the Father and the Son. Whoever denies the Son does not have the Father either; he who acknowledges the Son has the Father also "(1 John 2:22-23). The Jews denied the Son at the time of the crucifixion. In fact, they proclaimed *"Let His blood be upon us and our children"* (Matthew 27:25). The judgment that seems to fall upon these people is directly related to the crucifixion of Jesus.

But denying Christ goes far deeper than just the Jews. If we have any God other than Jesus, we are an infidel. Some people's gods are their children, for others it is their spouse, family, job, church, pension, security, etc. Or it could be their doctrine. Some even use the Holy Spirit for their own gain (Matthew 7:21-22). All these are of the antichrist.

Vine's New Testament Dictionary states the following: "The 'pseudo-christos', a false Christ is to be distinguished from antichrist. Pseudo-christos is found in Matthew 24:24 and Mark 13:22 The "false Christ" does not deny the existence of Christ, he trades upon the expectation of His appearance, affirming that he is the Christ. The antichrist denies the existence of the true God."

The antichrist is the person who places himself as god rather than Jesus. In a historical sense, the Roman Pope was called the "Vicar of Christ." Luther, Gibbon and others wrote that the word "vicar" means in place of. Thus, the Pope stood in place of Christ. This is an antichrist, one of many. As a side bit of information, there were two Popes who ruled at the same time for quite some time, one in France and one in Rome. At one point in time one Pope gave birth!

The beast in Revelation 13 is related to all of this concerning the antichrist. The 3rd verse of Revelation 13 reads: " I saw one of his heads as if it had been mortally wounded, and his deadly wound was healed. And all the world marveled and followed the beast."

Martin Luther mortally wounded the Roman beast with the Sword of the Spirit. He opened the Bible to the common man and thus began the restoration of the truth, the Holy truth. But the antichrist is still strong and healed. It was healed in order that those who would still desire deception would be deceived. For each is drawn away from God by his own lusts, whatever they may be (James 1:14).

For who can make war with the beast nature and win? It is only Christ. If we try to help the Lord win the battle, defeat is imminent. It is the Lord alone who wins the battle and will receive the glory! Paul strove with the beasts at Ephesus (1 Corinthains 15:32). These were not animals, but men who sought to preach another gospel, which was not the gospel of Jesus Christ. The beast nature rises up and produces the way of the flesh.

The antichrist is the religious beast nature within the breasts of the Christians who have not surrendered all to the Lord. The baptism of the Spirit begins the removal of the flesh if the saint yields to the Spirit, but if the saint does not, the flesh remains and controls the vessel, since the Spirit is gentle and will not dominate.

The son of perdition (2 Thessalonians 2), the man of sin, is responsible for the corruption of the world because he seeks to establish a "religious way " as acceptable. It was religion that ran the Inquisition, that Popish, diabolical plot to persecute true saints. It was religion that forced the Puritans and Pilgrims to flee for their lives from England. It was filthy religion that caused the Hugenots (French

Protestants) to flee France or remain and be killed by the Roman Catholic church.

Religion begat the crusades. The Popes needed money; the Western society needed an economic uplift. So religion led the way and self-righteously persecuted Moslems, who later retaliated and Western society felt indignant. In the history of religious Israel, religion destroyed the nation of Israel as Zealots challenged Rome. The religion of communism and the socialistic system battle Western culture's religious Judeo-Christian ethic. The struggle goes on for some.

While the son of perdition seeks to dominate, rule and control, the true sons of God seek to be humbled, to be made meek, and to be a servant. While the one elevates self, the other seeks to remove self. While one enjoys and seeks the limelight of notoriety, the other seeks to have the Lord glorified. While one seeks to be religious, the other seeks to be like Jesus.

The apostasy that we speak of is far larger than what is visibly seen on a world basis, national basis, or even a local basis. The apostasy is the man of sin standing up in the temple - in you.

Instead of God being seen in the house of God, we see the image of a false god - man. Jacob means supplanter or liar. He was a deceitful man. He slept at Bethel, which means in the Hebrew: house of God. His natural desires were stronger than God's. It was here he forced God, by the strength of the natural man, to bless him (he wrestled with an angel, Gen.32). On the way back from his trip, he now calls the place EL-BETHEL (Gen. 35:7) or God of the house of God. Jacob had yielded his nature over from being a liar, to the nature of God and his name was changed to ISRAEL which means one like unto God. God called Israel a rebellious house. So is the church the same.

The apostasy is being revealed. The rebellion has to be revealed before the manifestation of the sons of God. The harvest comes, and the angelic ministry of the reapers begins. The tares and wheat are harvested together. The tares mature faster and are sometimes taller than the regular harvest of wheat. But they are mutants. While they stand a "head" above the wheat, it is that very head that will be removed.

When the sons are birthed, the heavens are rent, even as the earth quaked with the death of Christ. For the graves, whited sepulchers, as the Pharisees were called, or vessels without water, will be opened and will show their apostasy. When their house, temple, is opened it will reveal either the fullness of Christ or it will reveal a dead corpse.

When real life is manifested, the apostasy will be truly revealed and understood for what it is! For a dead corpse will not look alive any more compared to a real live resurrected life. Who would choose the way of apostasy, if the way to true life were opened to them? The many faceted, multiheaded hydra of the god of self is being revealed for what it is. The beast rises (Rev.13) out of the sea, out of the humanity of man. The beast speaks platitudes that are at enmity with God, even blasphemous. *"Then he opened his mouth in blasphemy against God, to blaspheme His name, His tabernacle, and those who dwell in heaven"* (Rev. 13:6).

The antichrist denied that Jesus had come in the flesh (1 John 4:1-3). He looks for a physical appearing of Christ in the clouds. He denies the coming of Christ in a corporate body. Even the Jewish leaders of Jesus day denied that Jesus was the Son of God come in the flesh and called it blasphemous!

As it was then so is it now. Rather than fly away into some odorous cloud in a polluted heaven, we see Jesus coming forth in His sons (Romans 8:19-20). Meanwhile the beast seeks to rule from the heavens (our minds) masquerading under religious and spiritual power. Such is the war in the heavens that occurs with the birthing of the sons of God.

The very birthing of the sons causes the heavens to quake and that which is not of God, that which has no foundation in Him will be removed by the shaking. But God has a man who dwells in the heavens, lives in the temple, who shortly will be revealed after the apostasy has its full work.

To those saints who are pressing on for the high calling in Christ Jesus, be encouraged that God is moving mightily in you. For if you seem to see the beast nature, that carnal mind and any other corrupt thing before you, rejoice! The reason you see it is that the man of sin is being dethroned in you! God is moving in you. As He sits down to take His throne in you, He dethrones all that is carnal within you. So, what you see before your eyes is not what is in control but rather what God is moving out! Do not be deceived by the carnal mind which tells you that what you see is in control. It is not.

It is God that gives the victory. It is He arising in your temple, coming forth out of the ashes of the dead carnal nature slayed by the brightness of His swift coming to your tabernacle. Rejoice!

"But outside are dogs and sorcerers and sexual immoral and murderers and idolaters, and whoever loves and practices a lie."
Revelation 22:15

In Philippians 3:2 Paul writes concerning the Pharisees that they are "dogs." In chapters 5-7 of Matthew Jesus mentions that there are dogs which are hypocrites. The Lord implies there to the multitude that the "Pharisees" are such but He does not say that forthrightly. In Revelation 22:15 the word "dogs" is used again referring to the people OUTSIDE of Jerusalem.

Anyone who has known the way and receded is considered a "dog." Peter even writes that a dog will turn back to its own vomit and eat it. Repulsive. Repugnant. But a person controlled by his own desires and not willing for the Lord to remove those desires will turn again to the old way.

There are six things mentioned in Revelation 22:15. Symbolically, six is the number of man and the fullness thereof. But also note that there are three sets of two:

dogs - sorcerers   sexual immoral - murderers   idolaters - liars

There is a specific reason for the breakdown of these into three groups. Each represents a part of a person. We are all spirit, soul, and body. Each of these correlates to dogs-sorcerers, sexual immoral-murderers, or idolaters-liars.

It is obvious that sexual immorality and murders are related to the desires of the flesh, that natural plane. While there are indications it may be applied to the spiritual plane, the Scripture here would indicate otherwise because all three areas are covered individually.

Sexual immorality and murder can be forgiven - as in the case of David. Here we see a man after the heart of God who sinned but was forgiven. The sins of the flesh can hinder development of the individual but not keep the individual from entering into what God has for them.

Idolatry and liars are those who play mind games, things of the soulish realm. Generally, they set themselves up as the god of the house of God. Their desires, their goals and their purposes are superior to prevent the development of their families. Many raise their children to relive their own childhood in the way they wished it was for them. Idolatry is so subtle. Yet, it is also flagrant.

Idolatry was forbidden by the ten commandments (decalogue) in two specific ways. First, the people were to have no other gods before Yahweh. Secondly (Ex.20:4-6), they were to forbid the worship of any FORM of image or idol. Today this would take into account the idols: cross, image of Jesus, rosary, saint worship, Mary worship, pictures of the Lord etc. All these are outward or visible forms of idolatry.

This is one reason why Samuel was so upset that the people had to have a king. God was their king. But the people could not be spiritual enough to grasp that. They were so carnal that they had to have an icon in their house, or a king to look at. Today people have icons on their dashboards!

Idolatry is directly related to the carnal mind. For the carnal mind seeks to be religious. It seeks to be pure within the confines of an aesthetic nature. We find in Ephesians 5:5 and also in Colossians 3:5 that covetousness is a sin of idolatry. The desiring of "something" is a sin and keeps the person OUT OF the kingdom of God.

Paul writes that the children of light should walk in the light and abstain from the desires of the flesh and of the carnal mind. Both are at enmity with God. Both will keep a person out of the kingdom. The cost is too great for the pleasure of the very moment.

The key point though is that the covetous man is the same as an idolater. So, while the Old Testament dealt with the idea of literal idols and images, which are just as bad today, the New Testament deals more with the desires of the person.

The third area that the list includes is that of dogs and sorcerers. The word "sorcerer" is where we get our word "pharmacist" from. Not only does it mean the dispenser of drugs, but also means the magician, witch, or caster of spells.

Isaiah 56:10 states that false prophets are "dogs." Paul reuses that idea in Philippians. Here again we find that the "dogs" are outside of Jerusalem. That is to say that they are not in the household of faith which Jerusalem represents. In fact, Jerusalem represents *"the mother of us all"*(Gal.4:6) who are born of the Promised seed.

A false prophet is one who is religious but not of the same spirit as the ones in the faith. A false prophet is not one who prophecies incorrectly. There are many saints who know the spirit of the Lord upon them and do prophesy but taint it with some of their flesh. These are not false prophets. A false prophet is one who speaks out of the realm of the enemy. It is one who seeks to lead the people astray from Jesus Christ. A false prophet is tied to the antichrist and beast for he is of the same nature. His spirit is not of the Spirit of Christ.

Thus, when we find the usage of a "dog" in Scripture we find a reference to the spirit of the false prophet. The word dog/sorcerer refers to the spirit. Sexual immoralty/murderers refers to the flesh. Idolaters/liars refers to the carnal mind. All three levels of corruption are found outside the city of God. They have no part in the kingdom of God.

The dogs run to Gehenna, hell. They run to the refuse dump, which is what Gehenna means. It refers to the garbage dump outside the walls of Jerusalem at the time of Christ. The dogs, those false religious leaders, will go to the dump and eat the vomit of society, just as vultures eat the carrion of dead beasts.

The sorcerers are evident in society today. Drugs are the predominant form of self-worship there is. At the same time drugs show evidence of a self-hate, which is narcissistic in the sense that individual pleasure is most important, even at the cost of society. Yet, the very attraction of the drug is the very razor edge that slices the individual to destruction. Drugs are merely a symbol of the underlying problem in the culture.

Idolatry. It is the very substance of the carnal nature. It always sets itself up as God. Apostasy. It is the very nature of the carnal Christian. Whether the religious nature can be blamed on an organized church system or the individual is not the point. It exists. It exists because the fallen nature in man desires to rule whether in the religious, economic, social or personal level. The fallen nature is being removed as one becomes established in God. The seal now set on you is true. It is the seal of Christ, the very signet of His ring. He will rule and dethrone all that seeks preeminence in your life above Him. This is what the book of Revelation is about - the internal struggles of Christ to arise from your beastly, false prophet, antichrist nature. He shall and has, if you can hear that.

We have discussed the beauty of the revelation of Christ in us, the hope of glory. But before that true revelation can be made manifest, there must first be a falling away, a setting aside of the carnal ways of man that God might have the preeminence. This is accomplished by the revealing of the man of sin. 2 Thess. 2:3-4 states: *"Let no man deceive you by any means; for that day shall not come except there come a falling away first, that the man of sin be revealed, the son of perdition: who opposes and exalts himself above all that is called God...so that he sits in the TEMPLE of God, showing himself that he is God."*

The word temple here means your physical body and not a natural building as some would erroneously teach. The word here is the same as the temple that is spoken about in 1 Corinthians 3 where it says that your body is the temple of the Holy Spirit. The word "naos" is used in conjunction at all times with the natural body whereas; "heiron" is used for a physical structure.

What is the falling away? Standard teachings say that the falling away speaks of more people leaving the gospel and its teachings than are coming to it. We can clearly see the hardening of people's hearts. When the falling away is accomplished, then that which remains will be seen. First the earth is shaken, and all those false pretenses are let go. Then we find that the heavens are shaken and lo, the man of sin is revealed. When God begins to shake the heavens, all manner of angelic beings shall fall to the earth. They shall then begin to manifest their evil spiritual natures on the earth.

He is removing all things in the heavenlies that are at enmity with Him. There is a man of sin who sets himself up as God within the temples of men, and he sits in a spiritual place, living in our earth. We see him in saint and sinner alike. When we serve the flesh and the ways of death he rules. The very elect would be deceived except that the days are shortened. God consciousness has given way to religiosity. We deal with humanism at every turn.

The falling away and the revealing of the man of sin is not to scare or worry the Christian, but they should be received with rejoicing. Why? It is good so that the true saint can deal with those things in his life that do not measure up to the stature of the fullness of Christ (Eph. 4:12-13). You can not deal with a problem until it is exposed.

For when the fullness of his folly is manifest, then the Lord will appear glorified IN His saints (2 Thess. 1:10). The religious segment of the man of sin pushes for more traditions, rituals, rites and forms. Yet he denies the real power of godliness. The man of sin allows worship of the saints and praying to them; he favors pagan holidays; he preaches a legalistic faith and uses condemnation to control people; he tells others to stay in the denominations, preaches false doctrines of rapture, prosperity, seed faith and even prays for the dead. He preaches against the Lord's sovereignty by proclaiming man's free will. Oh, the church is full of the man of sin, and these religious ideas need to be flushed from the minds of the saints.

Blessed be God who allows this corruption to be revealed that the saints who are pressing on to know Him might step aside from such a miry mess and walk on solid ground. God has a people who have shaken themselves from man's corruption, and they will be the revelation of Christ to the world.

Chapter Ten

THE IMAGE OF CHRIST - THE SONS OF GOD

Most Christians are in Jesus Christ, but only some have experienced Christ Jesus. In careful study of the Scriptures we can see that Paul sometimes used the phrase "Jesus Christ" and at other times he said "Christ Jesus." The saint who is in Jesus Christ is saved and may be baptized in the Spirit. The saint who is in Christ Jesus has left his own carnality and is no longer bound by any man. For he who lives by faith and grace is not fettered. Some Christians have Jesus in them, but the deeper Christians are in Christ Jesus. Those in Christ Jesus are separated from the beastly nature and are past being carnal and at enmity with God.

The image of Christ is found in a person who has been conformed to the nature of Christ. Paul stated that he attained this, even while in this unredeemed body. In Galatians 1:16 he says that it pleased God to reveal His Son in him. The kingdom of God is found in the image of Christ. Christ was not of the earth, for He came from the heavens and had no part of Adam's nature Although He walked on the earth during His brief 33 years, He had His existence in that heavenly realm.

The kingdom realm is a spiritual realm with life that is hidden inside the Christian. Evil men have plotted to destroy it because this kingdom has caused great changes in the world situation. It is a controlling power which causes even unbelievers to do things they would not normally do. The power of the kingdom hardened Pharaoh's heart. It raised up Cyrus so that Israel would be released. This same power pervades the life of the Christian and can be exercised with his knowledge, or God can supernaturally use it without the believer's knowledge.

The saints who have the image of Christ are known only to God and have a special place in the purposes of the kingdom. These pure ones have the power to change history and the future, yet will not lift a pencil to do so if it be not His will. The person who is behind the scenes in the earth realm lives in the heavenlies with Christ and causes great changes in the earth. The earth would have been destroyed long ago if left to the unregenerated. The saints who have been conformed to the image of Christ act as the preserving agent. These hidden channels of life move the earth. The changes in the earth come from spiritual decrees, and only those who live in that realm have the power to accomplish the plans of God.

Consider the story of the pearl of great price. A man saw a pearl and asked what it would cost. The reply was, "This pearl will cost you everything." When asked what he owned the man responded that he had a house, a car, some cash and little else. The man soon learned that the pearl would require all of those things, his family and even his very life.

It is easy for us to give God something that is not too important to us. We may dedicate our house to the Lord and even give our possessions up for His use, but it is a little harder to give our families into His service. The hardest is to totally consecrate ourselves, crucifying all our desires until not one bit of the beastly carnal nature resides in our beings. We must give up ourselves in order to be conformed to the image of Christ.

Consider Joseph in Potiphar's house and how blessed that house was because of Joseph's presence. The world continues because there has always been a seed, a group of people who are being conformed to His image. They are the salt of the earth that preserves the very existence of its people. Joseph, chosen of God, brought salvation to Jacob and his sons (the household of faith) as well as to the families of the Egyptians (the world at large).

Yet, Joseph at that time didn't know why he was in Egypt at Potiphar's house, nor why he would go through more trials. He didn't wimper or complain; he just continued to believe that God was in control of his life, and he rejoiced in the path laid before him. Those called to be conformed to the image of Christ are in such a spiritual place that they go on with God regardless of the cost.

Such a hidden walk without an ostentatious or lavish show is not what most saints seek. I declare to you that the person being conformed to Christ does more than one with great exposure on the national scene in ministry. Some would be at ease in Zion and allow that beastly nature to run its course, but there are those who have had their flesh bow humbly before God and have ceased from fleshly labors. Their life in the flesh has been in total subjection to Him.

Oh, what a joy to receive a word of truth that "Your life is hid together with Christ in God," Col. 3:3. The elect's desire is to be totally separated from the beastly image and joined with Him forever. Those on the lower plane of existence cannot comprehend the depths of God. They can know about Him, but those of His nature have partaken of Him and dwell in Him.

The beastly image interprets the letter of the Word of God. Those of the image of Christ spiritualize the letter and it becomes life. As we have borne the image of the earthly, so shall we bear the image of the Christ. There is a first fruits company who will lead all creation into that higher plane.

Paul was caught up quite frequently in the Spirit and could finally say that the Son was revealed in him. Enoch was so possessed of the Christ that he "was not." The beginning of the end is at hand. The sons of God are feeling a finality transpire in their bosom. The manifestation is soon to be here for there have been more and more catching ups and the dealings of God seem to require a higher and higher level of holiness than ever before. Hear and understand. Those pressing on have been having experiences in the presence of the Lord which have been causing a great change as they behold His image more and more.

The kingdom of God can not be meat or drink but is spiritual. It is not healing a person to have him die of something else. The love of Christ constrains us so that we do not feed momentary life to this dead flesh. We are to be changed into His marvelous image so that we might be incorruptible and undefiled by that beastly image bearing death. The earth is on its last leg and in its death throes. But the sons are arising with the Morning Star ascending in their nature, and He is well able to change this vile creature into His image.

The Sons of God

The image of Christ is deeply founded in the Bible. There are many types of comings of the Lord, parousia, apocalypse, etc. Perhaps, at this point, we should discuss to a limited degree who are these "sons of God" found in Romans 8:19-20. With the understanding learned from this, it will make Revelation easier to comprehend.

Before we begin our study about the sons of God as found in the original Hebrew it is important to understand the <u>whole in comparison from the part</u>. The word "God" in English is a term used for the name of a deity. In our particular study the name "God" is used for the Christian God in contrast to the god of Mohammed, god of Buddah etc.

But even that word "God" reveals only a <u>partial</u> aspect of the deity. For in the study of the sacred Christian Scriptures we find that "God" has many names or manifestations. This also is true of each of us. At work you may be a supervisor or employee. You are a father or mother at home. In marriage you are a husband or wife. You are a child all of the time to your parents. Each of us is many things to different people; yet, we are a <u>whole</u> person, a composite of all these things.

So, also is the manifestation and name of God. He is revealed to us in the scriptures as "God," "Jehovah," the "I AM," "Jesus," and the "Holy Spirit." Each is a revelation of a certain part of His nature from which we are to glean the deepest of life.

While it is important to study the sons of God as mentioned in Romans 8:19-20, it is equally important to be well versed with all facets of the Lord's manifestation. We would recommend some excellent books to you to consider for your study concerning the nature of God: Andrew Jukes, **<u>The Names of God</u>**, **<u>What is His Name</u>** by John Green, **<u>God of Israel</u>** by David Cooper or **<u>Names of God</u>** by Nathan Stone. We also have a small booklet on the various names of Jehovah.

Assuming that you have considered and have done research on the various names of God, we shall consider only at this time His manifestation within the confines of "son of God."

"In the beginning God created the heavens and the earth."

Which beginning was this? It also says that the earth was already there without form and void, so we know that the earth had already been created. There are some theologians that think the creation of Genesis 1 is an actual second creation. Besides this point we want to know which facet of God we are talking about. The word "God" in the Hebrew is Elohim. El meaning God and "im" meaning one God with a plurality (Son and Holy Spirit). Rather interesting that the noun "God" is a singular but the verb is in the plural, which suggests the singularity and plurality of God (1:26). But in totally "poor" English!

Now there are many facets to God in the Bible. There is Jehovah. There is also El Shaddai, the "Almighty One" or "Full Breasted One" or the "One Full Of Life." El Elyon is the God of the kingdom age written about during the time of the kings of Israel. He is called the "Most High God." Another name we see is that of El Gibbor. Hagar saw this side of God when He revealed Himself to her in the wilderness. He "saw" her plight, and she called Him the God who sees.

<u>The word "God" is used at all times with the creation of the natural earth and natural heaven</u>. It is important to understand the concept that the name "God" is always used within the natural sphere of life. Thus, God is very intimately and lovingly involved with His own creation.

Through these examples we want to show that El (God) is in relationship to creation and the God of creation. But what happens when all creation is created? What happens when everything that has been created fully enters into His purpose in His unfolding plan? El becomes no more.

It is not that He is gone, it is that that facet or level of understanding of Him is no more - for some people.

How is that you say? As people mature in their faith in God, they begin to see a deeper understanding of His unfolding. He is no longer seen as a deity of creation only (most people recognize a "god" of creation), but also as a personal God. Let me further illustrate how we can see Him in a different vein or with a different understanding.

All persons, saved or unsaved, know that God is their creator, but they might not know Him as Jesus. Then upon coming to know Him as Jesus, they surely might not know Him as the one who baptizes with the power of 1 Corinthians 12 - the Holy Spirit. Some might never come to know Him as El Elyon. It is true that El Elyon is the Most High. <u>GOD IS NOT CONFINED TO ONE MANIFESTATION OR UNDERSTANDING</u>, but God is continuously revealing Himself to each person at the level that they need to see Him.

The man who sees God as his creator sees Him as a Father who begat him. If there is a starting point then there is an ending point. That facet of God is confined in time. When we enter into the fullness of His salvation, we do not need to experience that initial work anymore. The same applies to entering the fullness of Pentecost. You must move on from that realm. Even the precious revelation of the Father must be seen as a facet and not the ending place of our understanding of Him.

God has also spoken that He is the I AM. That aspect of Him is even bigger than the very revelation of Him as the Father because it is outside of time. The I AM is the "Living One" or "Ever Present One." This revelation of God is not bound to the earthly plane nor to our understanding of Him.

Let us see how far away He is! Revelation 20:11 speaks of the great white throne judgment. If we look at this verse in the traditional way, we see that the old heavens and the old earth are already destroyed, and there is a new heavens and a new earth.

"And I saw a great white throne, and him that sat on it, from whose face the earth and the heaven fled away; and there was found no place for them." We get excited when we think of a new heavens and a new earth. But here we see that no place can be found for either of them in the face of Him. We have a tendency to think that they were going to be fantastic places to be whether in the spiritual or the natural. But He says that even these are not close to Him! We think that the new heavens and new earth are something great because it is something that is close to us, but it is so far removed from closeness to Him that He can not even see it from where He is!

We get excited thinking we are moving closer to God in the new heavens and the new earth when we get our immortal bodies and redeemed minds. But I declare to you that it will never happen as long as we even have any type of body or mind. If we are tied to any natural plane we can not grasp Him in a fullness. He is SO large and SO great that man can not even comprehend what God is going to do. The redeemed mind cannot even comprehend it.

Look at the example of Christ. Jesus never used His mind. He had the total mind of Christ, that for which we are all seeking, and He never used it. He said that He did nothing except what He saw His Father in heaven do. He did only as He was led by the Spirit. We think we are spiritual when we have a redeemed mind, but we are truly not spiritual. Grasping things even with the redeemed mind is of no avail. Likewise making our minds a blank so that things can come in is also wrong. God wants us to use our minds to concentrate so that our spirits can be led of His Spirit and come into union with God.

The mind of Christ WAS LIMITED. He knew not the hour nor the time of the end of things - it was given to God He said. Luke 2:52 states that Jesus grew in stature and wisdom. But even He who was the very express image of God in the EARTH was LIMITED in His expression because He was no longer Spirit - but bound by time and the natural order of things while on the earth.

Thus, the natural heavens and the natural earth hinder a FULL revelation of God. This planet can express God, as found in Jesus, but it cannot express the fullness of God. The only fullness that will be seen is as much of the fullness that can be expressed in a vessel of creation. This automatically puts limits to that expression.

The manifestation of the SONS OF GOD is a tremendous revelation. But such a revelation is very closely tied to the earth, and thereby the revelation of the sons of God is limited in its scope. The manifestation of the sons of God as spoken of in Romans is to release CREATION from the bands and bounds of corruption.

The very function of the sons is to set free everything that is bound by the death throes of carnality. Their duty is to release creation from the old heavens and old earth into the NEW heavens and NEW earth. Such is the function of the sons of God (EL).

There are some that proclaim that they are already gods, however, such is not manifest in their lives. There is no drawing to these individuals as people were drawn to Jesus when He walked this earth. Also, if we follow the pattern, Jesus did not often openly declare that He was the Son of God. He revealed Himself personally to each individual.

He has called us to be like Him, and in order to do this one has to walk a thin red line - the Blood of Christ. Going off on the right or on the left will put you into error.

Coming forth right now is a Son of Man ministry, much as Jesus was on the earth. He demonstrated the Son of God ministry when He was crucified on the cross and in His resurrection. In Jesus' Son of Man ministry the people did not know who He was. Some of the more spiritual ones recognized Him as a prophet. But none knew who He was. He knew who He was.

This Son of Man ministry is to reveal the nature of Jesus within the confines of the natural body. Just as Paul stated: "It is no longer I that live but Christ that lives in me." Paul went on to say in Galatians 1:16 that it pleased God to reveal His Son in him. The Son of Man ministry is such that the vessel is not recognizable as being inChristed, even though it may be true. They didn't recognize Jesus even though He was the Son of God.

In comparison the Son of God ministry is not revealed until the end of the ministry and the crucifixion/resurrection. We are not speaking of merely having our old nature crucified. If that has not been dealt with, then we are not even in the New Man. Romans 6:6 says we WERE crucified with Him. We have already passed through that experience. Now it is a matter of putting on and revealing His Life. We are looking through the cross and to the resurrection, seeing the ascended Christ, our Lord Jesus who no longer is a man.

Jesus was slain from the very foundation of the world, and we were slain with Him in the spiritual sphere. Now it may be that we will be literally slain by persecutions to come, but that has nothing to do with us, because we are not our own anymore. We have already been crucified.

These persecutions should be as darts that we can take into us and push all the way through, because we are walking in light and they can not hurt us. We are not to ward them off, since we live in the kingdom order and can turn death into life, but are to take all things from the enemy and turn them back into life, because that is what Christ did. People who live in the church order, that Pentecostal order, use the shield of faith to ward off the darts of the enemy because they live in the heavens in which the enemy operates.

Our study on the Sons of Elohim will take us to the book of Ezekiel chapter 28 verse 2. We read of Lucifer here. There are many who say that Lucifer was a spirit, an evil spirit. However, as we read the following we see that he was a man and not a spirit:

"Because thine heart is lifted up, and thou hast said, I am a God (Elohim), I sit in the seat of God (Elohim) in the midst of the seas; yet thou art a man, and not God."

Adam stepped outside into a new realm when he said, "I am a God." He then separated himself from his god nature, that is, he divorced himself from God. That caused a division in the garden whereby God remained in the garden and Adam moved to his outer flesh and lived in his outer man. He then developed a relationship with the flesh and the outer man. God walked in the midst of the garden and said, "*Adam, where are you?*" But Adam was not there. He separated himself and was hidden because he lived in the outer man. So we see Lucifer as Adam in these verses. He was a light bearer. He was given a call, a word, a special anointing. (You might be interested in a tract that explains how Lucifer is Adam and not Satan).

If you have a <u>Strong's Concordance</u> you can look up the word "judge," and the number 430 is beside it. Upon looking that number up you see that the original Hebrew word for judge is Elohim. Looking at Exodus 22:8 we read: *"If the thief is not found, then the master of the house shall be brought to the **judges** (Hebrew Elohim translated other places as God) to see whether he has put his hand into his neighbor's goods."*

So we see that the man who does wrong is taken to the Elohim. In this case, the man who sinned was taken to one of the 70 judges appointed by Moses. The word "judge" in the KJV is the Hebrew "elohim."

This "Elohim" is a plural word. God, although singular, is also plural; while one, He is many. God as Elohim said, "Let US make man in OUR image." This we know to be the image of the Father, the Son and the Holy Spirit. We begin to come into the image of the Son through a born-again experience. We begin to come into the image of the Holy Spirit through the Baptism of the Spirit. Now we are coming into the image of the Father which is all Spirit. When God, El, spoke this in Genesis 1:26, He was speaking prophetically. For He even now is creating man in His image and is bringing forth Elohim. He called Adam to be Elohim. He wants them in the same image as Himself. Here we see God, who was a Spirit, the great I AM, the ever-present one, the ever-living one, who brings out a facet of Himself as El or God the Creator and says that He wants to make man in His image.

To clarify the point we must say that He did not say that He was making us in the image of the I AM. We can never be the I AM because we are created beings. We will always be less than what He is, but will always be ever growing in His nature. We need to come into what Christ had while He walked this earth. I believe that we will come into a total spiritual sphere. We will enter into Him unencumbered by a body.

As we come into the image of creator gods we can release creation from the bondage of corruption, thus fulfilling Romans 8:19. That is what He began through Jesus Christ for us, and the sons of God will finish it.

If we look at the judges mentioned in Exodus, we see men who had the power of life and death over everyone in Israel. God is calling a group to be the sons of God to have power over the house of Israel, over the brethren, the church, that they might become one. If we look at Luke 3:38 we see the genealogy of Christ. It reads: "*The son of Enos, the son of Seth, the son of Adam, the son of God.*" Adam was a son of Elohim. He had that relationship and the fullness of life. When he separated himself from that life God calls him a man rather than a son. God gave him a garment of skin, which is what we all are wearing right now. But thank God He has a plan to lift us up to what we had before the fall in order that we can ascend even higher than that. Genesis 4:25-26 reads:

"**and Adam knew his wife again and she bore a son and named him Seth. For God has appointed another seed for me instead of Abel whom Cain killed.**"

This seed that was newly appointed was a righteous seed. It was the son of God seed, for the lineage of Christ that we see in Luke comes from Seth. Look at how men called themselves at the time of the first generations. Genesis 4:26 states:

"And to Seth, to him there was born a son; and he called his name Enos: then began men to call upon the name of the Lord." or "then began men to call themselves <u>by the name of the Lord</u>." (literal reference)

Seth began to call himself what he was - a son of God. Many people in the 1600's had names like Johnson, which means son of John. Seth was doing nothing different than taking the identification of the name of Adam, son of God (Luke 3:38).

In Genesis 6:1-2 we see another reference to the sons of Elohim. *"And it came to pass, when men began to multiply on the face of the earth, and daughters were born unto them, that the sons of God saw the daughters of men that they were fair; and they took them wives of all which they chose."* These sons of God were not angels that cohabited with the daughters of men. They were men with a divine ministry who went down from that which they were called to and cohabited with the fallen nature. Thus God brought on the flood.

Eli's sons were also a type of the ministry falling and cohabiting with the lower nature, which was a step in the downfall of the nation of Israel. Eli, as a priest, was a type of God, Elohim. But his sons were wicked and even lay with women in the door of the tabernacle. He speaks to his sons in 1 Sam. 2:24-25:

"Nay, my sons; for it is no good report that I hear: ye make the Lord's people to transgress. If one man sin against another, the judge (Elohim) shall judge him: but if a man sin against the Lord, (Jehovah) who shall entreat for him?"

If the church sins, the sons of God, the Elohim can stand there and judge them. They rule with a rod of iron and they rule and reign in righteousness. Their purpose is to set things on a higher plane. Hosea 10:12 says that if you sow in righteousness you will reap in mercy. Galatians 6 says that he who sows to the flesh reaps corruption, but he that sows to the Spirit reaps eternal life. It is very carnal to think that if you sow to the Spirit you will reap prosperity. Eternal life is totally on the spiritual plane, not on the natural.

The sons of Aaron, as priests, were brought before the presence of God and killed by God through the fire of righteousness. They who were to be the judges of righteousness themselves had to be judged.

When the Elohim rule they do not do so with judgment unto death, but they in righteousness bring judgment with mercy in order to release that which God is raising up.

Exodus chapter 7 shows us Moses as a son in action. God says to Moses, "*See, I have made thee a god (Hebrew: Elohim) unto Pharaoh.*" If you have an understanding of history you know that the word "Pharaoh", whose name means "ruler of a great expanse," was viewed as a god and the high priest. Now Moses was told that he was Elohim (God) to Pharaoh.

In these last days God has a Moses company who reveal themselves as Elohim. They do so with dynamics because they have come into that relationship. They can go to the thresholds of the highest religious order, the highest political order, to the highest economic or social strata and proclaim a word that brings these orders down. They do not have to say what they are. They are what they are because of what He has done.

We know that the man Moses was the meekest man who lived on the face of the earth. The forty years he spent in the wilderness were not wasted. However, the spies spent forty days in the promised land, ate all the choice things, then refused to accept the light and truth of which they partook. Beloved, that is where we are today. We are eating of the seventh day and the new order. If it does not do its work in us, we will be buried in the wilderness like they all were. Two of the forty said that they could be sons of the Most High, and Caleb and Joshua both entered the promised land in their generation.

In the book of Acts chapter 28 we see Paul as Elohim. The snake came out of the fire and bit him, and he did not die. The people looked at him for a long time and reasoned that he must have been a god (Elohim). They repented and turned to this man's God.

Paul said, "*It is no longer I that liveth, but Christ that liveth in me, and the life I now live in the flesh I live by the faith of the Son of God who loved me and gave Himself for me*" (Gal.2:20). Paul no longer identified with himself but with Christ. In Galatians 6:17 Paul says, "*From henceforth let no man trouble me: for I bear in my body the marks of the Lord Jesus.*" These marks were not only from the whippings and persecutions he endured. He bore in his body the very sealing of the Lord, the fullness of the nature of God. This is what testified from his life. He had that relationship with God and was a son of Elohim. Even when left for dead three times, because his life was hid in Christ, he raised himself from the dead. Galatians 1:16 said the "Son of God" was revealed in Paul.

Jesus said of Himself in John 10:17, "Therefore My Father loves Me, because I lay down My life, that I might take it again. No one takes it from Me, but I lay it down of

Myself. I have power to lay it down and I have power to take it up again." Jesus had this power within Himself, given Him by His Father. So also Paul had entered into the relationship of the garden experience. He was one with his Father while having the same body that you and I have right now.

Finally we will look at a reference made by Paul in Galatians 4:14 and this should be the testimony of us all. *"And my temptation which was in my flesh ye despised not, nor rejected; but received me as an angel of God, <u>even as Christ Jesus</u>."*

What he says here is that the people did not look at his outer man. We know that he was an ugly, short man who had trouble with his eyesight and perhaps some arthritis in his hands from years of sewing tents, yet these people could look beyond that to the Christ that indwelled him to such a fullness.

Let it be said that the second coming had occurred in Paul's life. Likewise has God called us to be sons of God, Elohim, in this earth. It is a marvelous thing that He is doing in these last days. Let us go on to perfection. While we may become, even have the power to become (John 1:12) sons of God, this is merely one facet or expression of God, for He appears in many ways, even as a man might appear as a father, son, husband, etc. all at once. He is seeking to come and be glorified in His saints (2 Thessalonians 1:10).

Let us not forget, that the very thing that we look for, the manifestation of the sons of God, is not the fullness of God, but the fullness of God made manifest on the earth. We can never be the I AM. But we can be an expression of Him who has begotten us with such a lively hope. Then when we manifest Him in our being the world will see Him and seek Him who is Life.

Chapter Eleven

FIRSTFRUITS / ONENESS

One of the primary keys to the book of Revelation is understanding the union or wholeness of the Old and New Testaments. There is a sound that reverberates throughout the Bible that is a clear, distinct sound of the Lord's plan and purpose. Nothing stops this steamroller of God. His plan for the ages and the cosmos is complete, whole, and righteous. It remains for us to understand the plan of our Father.

In Genesis 1:1 we read the verse in the KJV as follows: *"In the beginning God created the heaven and the earth."* The Hebrew for the word "beginning" has in its meaning the word "firstfruits." So, we could read the verse as : *"In the firstfruits God created..."* Ponder this thought in the depth of your being. The firstfruit of the Father was His Son, the pre-existent Christ, that is, the Son in the Spirit before He made His earthly incarnation. Does not the Word proclaim that we were in Him from before the foundation of the world (1 Peter 1:19, Revelation 13:8)? It is found in Ephesians 1:4 which states: *" According as He has chosen us in Him before the foundation of the world that we should be holy and without blame before Him in love."* We can see then that Genesis 1:1 is expressed in Paul's thought of Ephesians 1:4.

The church was called out as a firstfruit of the world, even as Christ, the firstborn of all creation, was the firstfruit of the church. For just as Christ was birthed out of the Father, so all creation was birthed out of Christ which we find in John 1:3 which states: *"All things were made by Him; and without Him was not anything made that was made."*

Scripture declares that God is holy and that we are to be holy like Him. Since He is the firstfruit of the Father, then it follows that all that is created out of Him also has to be holy.

The pre-existent Christ was the firstfruit of God. The creation of Adam was a firstfruit of all creation. Jesus was a firstfruit of the faith spoken of in the Levitical offerings in Leviticus 23. The church, the true body of Christ - not any religious system - is the firstfruit of the earth that the whole will be brought in. Since we were chosen in Him from before the foundation of the world, we are to reveal the very nature of Christ. <u>This process of the revelation of Christ is seen or clarified in the book of Revelation, for it deals with the firstfruits coming into the revelation of Christ. View the book of Revelation from this perspective.</u>

Consider Adam from another perspective. In our writings over the years we have shown Adam as a type of Christ. Simply stated he was not deceived as Eve was (1 Timothy 2:14); he knew what he was doing. God had called him to oneness with God. To learn this Eve was given to him to teach him the oneness that he had with God. When Eve transgressed, Adam understood the principle of God needing to maintain the oneness. He crossed over and bore her sin on himself so that in the future she would be credited with producing the holy seed (Mary producing Jesus). He is a perfect type of the Lord. Recently, I came across a publication of 1843 where the brother expresses the same thought about Adam! James Reilly states: *"He voluntarily put himself into her condition, by receiving the fruit from her hand, and eating thereof: such was his love for his wife. And as they were not (though distinct in person) without each other in the Lord, <u>her</u> transgression extended unto <u>him</u>; and his **union** unto <u>her</u>, made it equitable for the curse and condemnation of her folly to fall on <u>him</u>; and that* *without the consideration of his consent and compliance with her."*

Adam understood the purpose of God - union, oneness. He like Christ gave his life for his wife even as Christ gave his life for the church, yea, even the world. Christ was not deceived. He knew what He was doing and why. Jesus understood the purpose of union and identification with us. He bore our sins in union with us. Adam bore Eve's sin in union with her. We need to come into such a union of oneness with God that our sole purpose is our identity with others. Just as Adam was never out of union with Eve, even so her sin affected him. So also Christ was in union with the church even though she sinned. The two are inseparable. Adam voluntarily placed himself in full identity with Eve and her transgression. Likewise Jesus did the same with the world. Adam knew, experienced his wife's frailties because of sin, so that he might bear her burden and judgment. Such union, such purpose is also seen in Jesus the Christ.

"For if the firstfruit be holy, the lump is also holy; and if the root be holy, so also are the branches." Now if the Father is the root, and the Son is the vine and we are the branch, the whole is holy for it is all begotten of the Father. However, it is stated a little differently in John 15:1. Jesus refers to his Father as the husbandman. The Father trims the vine (Christ) of branches that are not producing. Since all creation came out of Christ, God is trimming off those who do not produce the Christ nature. The effect of removing the non-productive branches enhances the ability of the remaining branches to produce more.

When I had heard the parable of the true vine, I always identified with the branches. Such a reaction is a natural selfish way of looking at things. When we look at the part (i.e. branches), we are carnal because we fail to see the whole. The Adamic nature always looks for itself, tries to find itself in the "picture." But the nature of God looks for the whole and the plan of the whole. We must see that God is moving with a holistic purpose. Read again John 15 and see the wholeness.

God tends the ground to prepare it for the inhabitation of His seed, the vine. The ground, the earth is representative of His whole creation of Genesis 1, as well as the man Adam who was without form and void. Then God's Spirit moved over the deep and in another location He breathed His Spirit into man. This is the hoeing of the ground (KJV helling). The Spirit plants the seed in the darkness, the earth. The seed from which the vine comes is Christ. For Christ is placed in darkness and darkness comprehended it not (John 1:5). This seed can produce only what it is. <u>The branches are PART of the whole and should not be focused on,</u> but should be seen only within the whole.

How serious is the problem of seeing only the part? I knew a man who was a homosexual. He had pictures on the walls and within his house. Let me give some background. The magazine *Playboy* reveals nude women as a whole. While it is not ours to discuss the viability of such a publication at this time, the key here is that it shows the whole person with a head, face and personality as well as a complete body. But the pictures on the walls of this man's house that I knew had only a certain part of a person's anatomy. The part became the focus unto total perversion. As saints we cannot focus on the part, the branches. We must place our gaze on the whole.

Perhaps this concept is a stretch for some personality types who like more details. Maybe a comparison between a Kiwi bird and an Eagle would be appropriate. The Kiwi is a

New Zealand bird. It has wings to fly but they do not work. It has a long beak and feeds at night by eating bugs that come out in the tall grass. The bird has no vision. If the field the bird was in caught on fire the Kiwi would find out by its beak being burned! It has wings but no ability to see above the current situation. But the eagle, soaring from the air can spot a fire a mile away. It is important that we see the whole and not the part, or that which is immediately in front of us. If we act or react from what is immediately in front of us, we fail to act properly. A proactive person sees the whole, the distant future, and plans accordingly; he is not affected by the current.

The husbandman is not concerned about the ground because he prepared it properly as part of a long-term plan. He is not concerned about the vine because he chose the best to come forth in production. He is not concerned about the bad branches because he knows this vine will produce the best branches. So, the husbandman removes the bad with anticipation of the best being seen shortly. God knows that the firstfruits are just that, firstfruits of what will come. So, God created in the beginning with the final expectation of what the firstfruits would produce - the full revelation of Himself.

There is a union not only of purpose begun with the "beginning" but a union of nature as well. *"Of His own will begat He us with the word of truth, that we should be a kind of firstfruits of His creatures."* God planned from the foundation a manifestation of His firstfruits which started with the pre-existent Christ.

The union of God and creation starts at the beginning, which is also the ending. God creates from the firstfruits so that all will be summed up in Him in the end (1 Corinthians 15:25-28). God's goal is the end, the final product, if you will. To accomplish the end, He has selected a firstfruits company founded by His Son to establish the end result, manifest it first, and bring it to a conclusion. The nature of the firstfruits is identical with the nature, character, of God.

Exodus 23:19 states: *"The first of the firstfruits of thy land thou shall bring into the house of the Lord thy God."* The firstfruits are the offering that is acceptable to God. Jesus was acceptable as a sacrifice to God not only because He was God's son, but also because He was the firstborn of all creation. He established a heavenly man in a natural realm (1 Corinthians 15:44-49). Thus, He could be the propitiation for our sins because of who He was - the firstborn of a new creation.

Isaiah 46:10 reads in the KJV: *"Declaring the end from the beginning (Hebrew firstfruits), and from ancient times the things that are not yet done, saying My counsel shall stand and I will do all my pleasure."* The end is based upon the beginning or as the Hebrew states, the firstfruits. If the firstfruits are not in proper order, all is failure. If you were to draw a line and it was not completely straight, say just off one-quarter of an inch, within a mile you would miss the mark or location you wanted by over 200 feet.. It has to be perfect. The pre-existent Christ was/is. The pre-existent Christ lowered Himself a little lower than the angels and appeared as Jesus and was the perfect man.

God has called a firstfruits from the earth who are redeemed from men (Revelation 14:4). These are those who stand before the throne. They stand because they have entered into His nature. They do not have to bow down as some do because they are standing in His nature and not their own! As Isaiah 46:10 states it may not appear that the Lord has things under control, but do not be deceived.

"Things may not yet be done" as the verse states but that is not to be confused with the thought that the way things are is the way they will be.

"The fear of the Lord is the <u>beginning</u> of wisdom" states Psalm 111:10. How often that verse has been quoted and received with rejoicing. Yet, the word "beginning" is the same word that is found in Genesis 1:1. So, let us read that again this way: *"The fear of the Lord is the <u>firstfruit</u> of wisdom."* Christ was the first fruit. It is only as we enter into union with Him Who is the only firstfruit that wisdom begins. Oh, let me say that again in another way for the importance of it cannot be lost! He has the only true identity. Adam's identity is a lie, deception. There is no life but His. We do not have a life which we share with Christ but rather His life is ours. (Even that statement - His life is ours - reveals duality which there is not.)

As firstfruits we reveal the original firstfruit. Proverbs 8:24 speaks of wisdom when it states: *"I was set up from everlasting, from the <u>beginning</u>* (firstfruits) *or ever the earth was. When there were no depths, I was brought forth."* Where was wisdom? In the beginning, the very foundation of all that was created. Wisdom was Christ and we were in Him. Proverbs 8:21 states: *"That I may cause those that love me to inherit substance; and I will fill their treasures."* The word "treasure" found in Exodus 19:5 which is similar to Peter's quote in the New Testament when he speaks of "treasure" which means a storehouse. Consequently, those that love the Lord, the firstfruits, will have their void, their armory, their storehouse filled with the <u>substance</u> of wisdom, which is Christ Himself.

Christ is married to the church. We need to comprehend the depth of this mystery. As a husband and wife become one in spirit, soul and body, so then all that they do is the appearance of one. Since our identity is in Him Who is the firstfruit, the One who will bring all things into Himself, we must also function in like manner. This brings the restoration of all things spoken of in Acts 3:21.

Job was a blessed man of the Lord. He had a wonderful family and his first family was, as it were a firstfruit. Because of his trials he lost all he had including his children. *"So the Lord blessed the latter end of Job more than his beginning* (firstfruits)." Job had in the latter end seven sons and three daughters as in the beginning. It took the firstfruits in Job's life to produce the latter end. It took the righteous nature of God in His life to enlarge Him. **Christ, being of the nature of God, the firstfruit of God, will enlarge the revelation of the nature of God**. Since we are seed of His seed, begotten out of Him we also will assist in the revelation of God. Thus, the glory of the latter house is greater than the former because it has been enlarged.(Haggai 2:9). Firstfruits are merely an indication of the crop that follows.

A farmer rejoices at the firstfruits because he knows what will follow. He shouts for joy at the firstfruits not because of them but because he knows they indicate the harvest that is about to take place. Sometimes I think Christians are hunters rather than farmers. They are always hunting - trying to find the one that needs to be saved. Hunters seek out one but do not stop to plant and raise. Hunters get excited and rejoice over one that they "bag" for the Lord. The vision of the hunter is for the immediate - that which is presently before their eyes. The farmer, on the other hand, looks for the end result and sees the firstfruit as confirmation that the end will be just like the beginning. The farmer sees the whole because he has a vision of a mature field even when he plants a tiny seed. God preferred the offering of Abel over the hunter. Not that the hunter's offering was bad, but the attitude of the hunter was open to question. But we, like Abel, need to be farmers and cultivate the seed that is already in the vessel and allow it to come forth in the field given to us. The harvest field is white and ready. It is time for the firstfruits to begin that harvest.

"Of His own will begat He us with the word of truth, that we should be a kind of firstfruits of His creatures." It is out of His will that the firstfruits come. They can do nothing but the performance of His will because they have been conformed to His nature. There can be no other truth than the one purpose of God - to manifest Himself in all creation. This presents the unity of it all. For who has seen the complete work of the Lord but Him who saw the end from the beginning or the end from the firstfruits of it all.

The "word" of truth in the Greek is Logos. (See our message on the Logos for the greater detail of the truth of "Logos".) But suffice it to say that the Logos is the revelation of the divine expression made manifest in the earth. The Logos not only spoke it all into creation but spoke Himself into the creation as the manifestation of Jesus. He came to set men free that they might through Him become one with Him and the Father.

Out of the Father's will. Think about that phrase. Out of the Father's will. The will begat us. The will is a means of creation. Carefully ponder what I am about to say. The Father is masculine - able to place His will (seed) so that it can begat. Now, He begat us through the word of truth. The "word" is the Logos, which is His Son, the pre-existent as well as the physical manifestation. His Son carries us in His womb to deliver us up to the Father as a firstfruits to the Father. The firstfruits are acceptable to the Father and therefore the whole field, the children that follow out of His womb, are acceptable. Oh my, what a precious life this is!

Now we know that the tares grow up with the firstfruits until the time of harvesting the firstfruits. Then the difference is noticed. As we read the parable of the 30, 60, 100 fold we find that the seed that is sown is Christ (Luke 8:11). Christ sows Himself into the earth, the Adamic creation, us. The seed of Himself is already acceptable to the Lord, His Father. Thus, Christ who birthed all creation out of Himself (John 1:3-4) established beforehand that the firstfruits would be acceptable. So, in the plan of God Christ is in the process of creating sons who are of His seed.

How good is this seed? Jacob says of Reuben, his firstborn: *"Reuben thou art my firstborn, my might, and the beginning* (Hebrew firstfruits) *of my strength, the excellency of my dignity, and the excellency of my power."* While we know that Reuben was a man from a man and not a perfect type unto us, yet we can draw life from the statement that Jacob makes for it is true of all firstfruits.

There is in every man an amazement at the power to procreate. The ability to give life is just as powerful to a man as it is for a woman to carry and birth a child. When the child comes the world gives much glory to the woman and deservedly so. But the man is greatly left out of the picture. He too is overpowered, overwhelmed at the birth of a child because he realizes the strength of himself and what it means.

It is no wonder that Jacob looked at Reuben all the time and thought of his firstborn with great consideration regardless of the frailities of that man. Every look at his son brought to Jacob the thought of the remembrance of God coursing through Jacob and empowering Jacob with the ability to give life. So, too, Jesus was ecstatic over the firstfruit of His loins and the possibilities. The plan of the ages would be complete because the firstfruits were birthed and had been conformed to His image.

"These are they which were not defiled with women; for they are virgins. These are they which follow the Lamb whithersoever He goes. These were redeemed from among men, __being the firstfruits__ unto God and to the Lamb." Rev. 14:4

These were not defiled with women. What does that mean? As one studies the word, we find that Eve was deceived. Eve came out of Adam. He represents the spirit and she the soul, the feminine. The word "psuche" in the Greek is feminine and is used for the soul. These 144,000, the firstftuits, were not defiled by the carnal mind. They had no relation with it. No marriage was made, that is, the carnal mind was not allowed to consummate its fleshly desires.

The spiritual nature of the firstfruits was not beguiled by the fleshly nature of Proverbs 7. The writer of Proverbs states clearly that Wisdom (ie. Christ or at least the Holy Spirit) was to be the man's sister. The carnal mind tries to seduce the young man. If it does, the individual must walk a path that is far more arduous than if union were maintained with the family of God. These were virgins it states. Virgins because they had not given themselves over to the temptations of the desires of the flesh.

The firstfruits did not prostitute themselves for a moment's pleasure. They decided to use the Spirit of the living God in them to "keep" them from evil as 1 John 5:18 states: "*...he that is begotten of God keeps himself and the wicked one touches him not.*" They follow the pattern that Jesus set before them. Jesus in Matthew 4 is led of the Spirit into the wilderness (read our booklet about the Wilderness) to be tempted. He in His temptation did not identify with the temptation but identified with the nature of God in Himself and thereby overcame the temptation. So too, the firstfruits. They are so focused on who they are in Christ that they cannot be drawn away from their identity - for their life is hid with God in Christ. This is the difference between the firstfruits and the others who follow after them.

How else could they follow the Lamb wherever He goes if they did not keep their eyes on Him? It is because their focus is on Christ that they have the victory. When you walk with Christ you have fellowship with one another as you are in the light (1 John 1:7). In Him there is no darkness at all. One cannot get lost, cannot fall out of the light into darkness if he walks in the union of the Spirit of 1 Corinthians 6:17, because he that is joined to the Lord is one. In fact this word "join" is the same word "made" in the KJV of Ephesians 2:14. He has made us one by removing the wall that was between us. They can follow the Lamb because the skin, the face that covers the deep, has been removed from them.

We note that these were "redeemed from among men." The word "redeem" means to have been bought. Once bought the ownership of the thing determines where it resides, lives and dwells. Christ has bought us and placed us in the realm of life for us to walk in. Salvation is for the soul in that Jesus offered His soul for the Adamic soul (Isaiah 53:10). Redemption is given for the deliverance of the body, the natural body. Paul writes how there is a house within our natural house (2 Corinthians 5, see our audio tape). When the time comes the earthen, this Adamic, will be removed and the inner nature and the inner house, not made with hands will appear. There have been men who have seen it from afar (Hebrews 11:39-40), who possessed it by the Spirit ("kairos" time) but it was not the appointed time ("kronos" time) to manifest it.

Consequently, there is a cloud of witnesses, people from times past that are a firstfruits company waiting for the sons of God of Romans 8:19 to manifest - apocalypse, unveil, reveal the complete revelation of Christ. The sons of God are the last who receive the same payment as the firstfruits of previous ages.

But let us take a moment to consider the cost of being a firstfruit. It takes being cut off from the source of life that you have had, even as Jesus was cut off from the Father on the cross for the sake of others. Yet, it means also that the life in you, that Christ life, is powerful enough to deliver you from the cross, such a union! The firstfruits are to be a sacrifice so that others can enter in - a bridge that others can feel free to walk on. The firstfruits are "crypt-kickers," that is, they have conquered death and no evil thing can hurt them even if it takes their natural body. Death cannot touch them because they have been harvested into life by allowing the dying of the Lord Jesus in their body (2 Corinthians 4:10).

Rejoice ye firstfruits. Oh clap your hands all you people for there is One who is the Way, and He has prepared a firstfruits who are a pleasing savor unto Him. It is these who have come out of the fire and have no smell of smoke from the lake of fire on them. They have overcome. He is their God and they are His son - Revelation 21:7 - the eighth level, the new beginning of overcoming.

Chapter Twelve

Lamb or Lambkin?

John wrote 5 books of the Bible. In the gospel of John, chapter 1 verse 29, he writes, *"Behold the Lamb of God."* Jesus was the Lamb of God. Peter writes that Jesus was the Passover lamb without spot or blemish and thereby was sacrificed as the perfect Son of God in order to be the propitiation of our sins.

In the Old Testament the pattern was set where the high priest would offer a lamb, the firstling of a flock, without spot or blemish for the sins of the nation. The appearance of Christ did away with the annual sacrifice that was required, because He became the once-and-for-all sacrifice. Therefore, there is no longer a need for the ordinances of sacrifice to be continued.

Now this word "Lamb" used in 1:29 is only used three more times in the New Testament. The other occurrences are found in John 1:36, Acts 8:32 and 1 Peter 1:19. All the other 31 times where "lamb" is used (thirty times in Revelation) the word does not refer to Jesus specifically, but possibly could by implication.

The Greek in all these other occurrences means "lambkin." In other words, the "lambkin" means a company or group of lambs or a diminutive term for lamb. The many places where this occurs in the book of Revelation cause a tremor in the normal interpretation of the book, but also enliven the true meaning.

"Then I looked and behold, a Lamb standing on Mount Zion and with Him 144,000 having His Father's name written on their foreheads." Revelation 14:1

Mount Zion is the location used in Psalms for describing the highest realm in God. In relation to it we see Israel as a type of feast of Passover or first time experience with God in salvation. The city of Jerusalem in Israel represents in type and shadow the feast of Pentecost or the baptism of the Holy Spirit in 1 Corinthians 12. Within Israel and within Jerusalem is Zion or the feast of Tabernacles which represents the third experience of union with God.

The 144,000 which some interpretations take literally, is an allegorical number - a square of the number 12. Throughout the scriptures, the number 12 refers to divine government: 12 tribes, 12 gates in the city, 12 disciples. So in this verse we see that these were those who are governed by the laws of the kingdom of God and not subservient to the laws of men.

The verse further states that they had the name of the Father in their forehead. This also is important. Jesus is the way to God, salvation. He came that He might send the Holy Spirit to lead us into all truth (John 16:13). Jesus baptizes us in the Spirit with the gifts of the Spirit. But the Father's name refers to the third experience, entering into a relationship with the Father.

This means that these 144,000 have become fathers in the Lord. They in their own way are able to produce life on the spiritual plane because of the union that they have with the Father. We are not just talking about leading someone to the Lord, although that is part of it, but rather these people are able to birth people into all three feasts - Passover, Pentecost and Tabernacles.

Now the Father's name was written on their foreheads because this signifies that each saint has the mind of Christ, even as the priest in the Old Testament had the golden name plate held on the forefront of the turban by twine that was made of blue thread and written on it was *"Holiness to the Lord"* (Exodus 28:36-38). The blue speaks of a heavenly order. These who have the seal of God are those that have entered into the nature of God and have become the "huios," the sons of God.

As we look at this verse we note that there is a Lambkin standing on Mount Zion with Him (Him is referring to Jesus). As we noted earlier the word Lambkin means a diminutive or lesser in the sense of smaller lamb. While many have been conformed to His image over the years, none will be like Him because He is the only Begotten of the Father. Nevertheless, He is our Elder brother, which means we are like Him. Confusing but true!

"But I saw no temple in it for the Lord God Almighty and the Lamb are its temple... and the Lamb is the Light" Revelation 21:23

The New Jerusalem is what is being discussed here. You are the temple of the Lord. The Lambkin is the Light. The truth of this verse is magnificent. I would that all could search the depth of this verse.

The lambkin is, as discussed already, a smaller, lesser but the same as those who have come into His image. The City as discussed earlier is the bride of Christ, the church corporately and individually

There are many firstfruits in Scripture, even as Christ was a firstfruit, and there will be those who will be a firstfruit in His image also. These are those who have been beheaded, losing their Adamic identity for the government, the headship of Christ and the kingdom of God. These firstfruits then become the habitation of the Most High and He illuminates out of them. Effectively, they become the lambkin.

But it goes even further if one can grasp the beauty of the Lord. 1 John 4:20 states: *"If someone says, 'I love God' and hates his brother, he is a liar; for he who does not love his brother whom he has seen, how can he love God whom he has not seen?"* If you cannot see God in the other person, you only see the Adamic nature, that fallen nature and you cannot love God.

But if you do see everyone in Christ, then the nature of Christ that you find in everyone can minister through you and to you. So, when it states that the Lambkin is the light, it is referring to the whole body of Christ, corporately but more importantly individually. For each individual is to be so joined to the Lord that each person is one (1 Corinthians 6:17). Now, if I am totally in union with God and you are totally in union with God yet maintaining our own personalities, then we are one, are we not? Therefore you light my city and I can light yours. We can flow from vessel to vessel because it is His Spirit that makes us one.

Lest any would fear that I am talking about evil spirits, or even allow evil spirits to flow through me, please lay the book aside and pray. What I am stating, if one can hear it and some cannot, is that God flowing through each individual can also flow through you at the same time with the cloud of witnesses to empower you with His nature. This union of purpose, this oneness of Spirit through our savior Jesus Christ which can only be done through Him, is an apocalypse of His coming.

"And I looked, and behold, in the midst of the throne and of the four living creatures, and in the midst of the elders, stood a Lamb as though it had been slain, having seven horns and seven eyes, which are the seven spirits of God sent out into all the earth." Revelation 5:6

Scripture declares that we have sat down in heavenly places with Christ. Even as He sat down with His Father on His throne, we have sat on the throne with Christ (Rev.3:21). The word "lamb" here again, as in all of Revelation is lambkin. Note it <u>was not</u> slain. Jesus was slain from before the foundation of the world (Rev.13:8, 1 Peter 1:19), but this lamb <u>appeared to be slain</u>. There is a vast difference. So, this is not Jesus here who was the sacrifice for us and the only one needed, but the ones conformed to His image make up this lambkin.

The seven spirits of God listed in Isaiah 11:2 are: Spirit of the Lord, wisdom, understanding, counsel, might, knowledge and the fear of the Lord. Note that these spirits are sent out into all the earth - the Adam man, not the planet earth. Horns speak of authority and power. Seven speaks of completeness. Thus, this lamb looked as though it had been slain because it identified itself with Jesus and had the fullness of Him within its vessel.

It is the corporate expression of God found in the lambkin. There is nothing more pleasing or beautiful to God than when the brethren dwell together in unity because it manifests the glory of God. The individual must possess his own reins, but also must be able to flow with God's other vessels to bring the full manifestation of God in the earth. Life flowed out of Jesus because He was in perfect harmony with the will of the Father. The sons of God must also be in perfect harmony for the life of God to manifest through them. Praise God for the Lambkin company.

"These will make war with the Lamb and the Lamb will overcome them, for He is Lord of lords, and King of kings; and those who are with Him are called, chosen, and faithful." Rev.17:14

The people who have not yet experienced Christ as their savior still reside in their Adamic nature, that fallen nature. They make war with the lambkin - the individual members and the body of Christ as a group. But it takes the company of the brethren to overcome them; we cannot stand alone in the face of a trial. It takes the body of Christ to encourage us. Even in the natural, when the toe is cut by a sharp rock, the pain is excruciating, but the brain is consoled because it knows that it will pass. The toe, however, has no concept of that! It takes the whole body to bring balance and support when another is under attack.

The strength in numbers offers encouragement to the individual to accomplish the task set before him. Many in the first century were persecuted unto death, and they finished the faith because they drew strength from the other brethren. We have fellowship with one another as we walk in the Light - which you are. It is time that the Lambkin recognizes its brethren rather than dividing within itself creating a cancer rather than life.

"Be of good cheer, I have overcome the world," states Christ in John 16:33. Since we are alive in Him we too can manifest the overcoming nature multiplied many times as we find our identity in others - in the Christ in others. Be not dismayed, for we have overcome through Christ Jesus our Lord and it is experiential.

Chapter Thirteen

One Like Unto

"And I looked, and behold, a white cloud, and on the cloud sat One like the Son of Man having on his head a golden crown, and in his hand a sharp sickle." Revelation 14:14

The word "one" does not exist in the Greek as a word but is implied within the context. The concept of "one" is a corporate concept, not an individual. The question then is who is the "one"? Careful study will reveal to the individual that it is the true body of Christ, the church (not a building but those who walk after the Spirit of life in Christ Jesus).

This "one" is located in the heavens which the cloud represents. The key here is that there is no identification with the earth nature, the nature of Adam but a complete identification with the heavenly man, Christ Jesus our ascended Lord whose image we are now putting on (1 Corinthians 15:47-49). Flowing with life from the heavenlies this "one" now becomes the appearance of the "Son of Man."

The key word in this verse is "like unto". Not that the "one" is the Son of Man because there was only one, Jesus. But this corporate expression of the body of Christ appears "like unto" the Son of Man. The Greek means "similar to, but not the same as." We can never be Jesus simply because He is always revealing a greater depth of Himself to us, but we are forever growing into His nature and consequently can reveal Him to others.

This "one" is a corporate Son of Man. Each person comprises a part of the whole. In essence, each person must come into the depth of the revelation personally which causes the manifestation of the corporate expression of the Son of Man. This is one way that we shall do "greater works" than Jesus did.

Note that this "son of Man" had a golden crown on his head. This again ties back into Revelation 14:1 where the Father's name was written on their foreheads. The golden crown speaks of divinity, purity, holiness, righteousness. The mitre set on the head of the "son of Man" is a confirmation that the body it is set on has come under the full divine government of the Lord. The kingdom order rules their own personal lives as well because they submit one to another in love.

I might interject here that this is occurring today in two ways. In every generation since Christ there has always been a remnant that has seen and possessed this (Hebrews 11) but they are waiting for a critical mass to occur so that they might join with those of the 42nd generation who manifest this. If enough do not participate, then the current day remnant will pass on and await in the spirit for those who will manifest it. The cloud of witnesses enjoins us to press our way into the "Son of Man." Secondly, if you can see by the Spirit the truth of discerning the Lord's body (we have a small booklet on that subject), you can join with others that might manifest the day of the Son of Man.

It is important to note that the "Son of Man" refers to Jesus before the cross; when He revealed His "Son of God" nature was at the resurrection. Many are familiar with the concept expressed in Hebrews that Jesus was prophet, priest and king. Up to the time of the cross, Jesus was considered a prophet, a carpenter's son, etc. He revealed His priestly ministry on the cross. He was not considered the Son of God because the people could not discern it. Thus, this

"Son of Man" ministry is a heavenly ministry even as Jesus' was a heavenly ministry, but it is a ministry where people do not recognize you as a son of the Most High (Romans 8:19-20). It is a hidden but profitable ministry, for the kingdom and God knows who you are, even if the people do not. Selah (Sit and ponder that).

"and in the midst of the seven lampstands One like unto the Son of Man clothed with a garment down to the feet and girded about the chest with a golden band" (Rev. 1:13)

Here again the "one" does not refer to Christ Jesus but rather to those who have been conformed to the image of the Son of Man. In fact, a close scrutiny of the difference between the "Son of God" and the "Son of Man" can be enlightening. Basically, the difference is that Jesus walked as a man, hidden until He revealed His sonship on the cross and in the resurrection. For thirty-three and one-half years Jesus walked as a man. People considered Him a prophet. He revealed Himself as a prophet during His ministry. He was revealed as a priest while on the cross and then manifested his kingship in the resurrection.

The "Son of Man" ministry is what the "one" reveals. In other words, these particular saints who formed the corporate expression of Christ in the earth have died to the Adamic nature. They now know that their life is hid with God in Christ and serve a risen Savior. They know this experientially and not just with cognitive ability.

Jesus walked the earth without ever yielding His members to anything that was carnal or of the Adamic nature. These who have come to know that truth fulfill 1 John 5:18, 20b. There is no longer a battle within their vessel between good and evil, right and wrong, or as the Eastern religions call it - yin and yang. The corporate expression of Christ walks within the confines of His nature and is not frustrated about what is going on in the natural because their desire is to fulfill the plan of God, even as Jesus did.

The "Son of Man" ministry is one that leads to the manifestation of the cross. But if one did not have the life before the cross occurs, death would reign. Thanks be to God, that we can live in Him and yet, though we go to the cross for others' sakes, follow His pattern (Philippians 3:17, 1 Peter 2:21), we are victorious because we do not live in the outer man who is perishing. We use the outer man as a seed so that the inner man, a heavenly creation, can be revealed. This "one" is a group of saints who have recognized that they are alive unto Christ and freed from the law of sin and death.

This "one" is within the seven lampstands. The lampstands, all theologians agree, represent the seven churches. The discussion between theologians is whether the churches are past or future. We shall not consider that but rather apply the verse spiritually. We, the saints, are the church. It is not some building at some historical or futuristic time. The "one" stands in the middle of the church. With the body of Christ there are many levels of Christianity. Some are babes, some adolescents, some adults. Within this body is a remnant called to the "center.+
" These are those who have been conformed to His nature. Not all Christians have such an aspiration.

Not everyone is a David Brainerd, John Huss, Mother Theresa, Smith Wigglesworth, etc. Not everyone will lay down all that they are in Christ so that they can be a bridge for someone else to walk over into the realm of life. Within the body of Christ is a remnant. These are those, disguised by the frailties of the flesh, who like Jesus are not discerned for who they are. These saints, like Jesus walk undisclosed before people. People cannot discern who they are just as they could not discern Jesus. In fact, this fulfills 1 John 4:2-3. The **Lord has come in the flesh of the saints to be glorified in them** - 2 Thessalonians 1:10.

This "one" in the center of the lampstands is Christ in His corporate manifestation. He is the head and we are the body. It is when the body of Christ discerns who they are rather than believing the lie that they are in Adam and hope to have a change when they get to "heaven", then and only then will the bones of Ezekiel 37 get sinews on them and the Lord arises from the ashes of those dead in Christ.

"Immediately, I was in the Spirit; and behold, a throne set in heaven, and One sat on the throne." Revelation 4:2

Heaven is where God is. Our small booklet (The Real Location of Heaven and Earth) tries to explain that scripture clearly shows that God dwells in heaven and He is within the individual. Heaven is not a geographical location but rather a spiritual realm. The "one," that corporate expression of Christ, is in heaven and therefore within the breast of the saint. Paul was encompassed about with a great cloud of witnesses. He saw them as a support group because he was in the same realm as they. The three disciples discerned Moses and Elijah on the Mount of Transfiguration with Christ because they had their spiritual eyes open. Elisha opened the eyes of Gehazi so that Gehazi could see that they were protected. All these leaders entered a realm and became one with the living Host.

Christ has called us to become one with Him (1 Corinthians 6:17). Such union brings us into union with the body of Christ. Through Christ we become one with another.

We no longer walk with the eyes of Adam but walk through the eyes of Spirit, seeing things as though they are. It is only as I see you as a manifestation of Christ, that I can love God. Consider 1 John 4:20 which states: *"If a man say, 'I love God' and hates his brother, he is a liar: for he that loves not his brother whom he has seen, how can he love God whom he has not seen?"* Christ gave Himself for the church, even as we give our life for God by laying it down for the brethren. As I love my brother, I love Christ who in reality is my brother.

We only begin to sit on the throne as part of the "one" because we understand the principle of our Father. Our God is one and we are called to see all things in Christ that *"in the fullness of times he might gather together <u>in one all things in Christ</u>, both which are in heaven and which are in the earth, even in Him."* Philippians 2:10 adds "<u>and under the earth</u>." Only as we see the oneness of purpose can the body become one with the head of all things.

A throne is a position of authority. Such a position has authority only because the one in the position realizes that he is a servant of all and has one purpose. That purpose is to bring all in the kingdom into harmony where peace reigns. This can only occur when there is a firstfruits company who has defeated the enemy of death and walks in the realm of life, who is the Lord (John 14:6). This corporate expression of "one" has not only entered into who He is, but has partaken of His life and rules by the laying down of Him who is their life in them. In effect they cut themselves off from the one they love by giving their life for others. This is oneness with Christ!

SUMMARY

This book while finished is yet under construction because the purpose is to present each saint as a living epistle read of all men. Growth requires change, openness, consideration and reading between the lines.

My prayer is that you have caught the Spirit behind this book and not the letter. Spiritualizing the Bible, after understanding it on the natural and historical plane, empowers the spiritual life. It was not until I understood the Scriptures in a new light that my relationship with God increased.

When I realized that Jesus Christ is the Savior of all men, especially those that believe (1 Timothy 4:10, Psalm 22:27,29, 1 Corinthians 15:22, Romans 5:15-17), I began to see that life of Christ could come out of my temple and assist in the plan of salvation and redemption that 99 would not be saved, but all 100 lambs. The only way for the world to see Him is if I let them in His temple and I let the body of Christ, my brethren, to be joined unto me as we are joined unto Him.May this book be life unto you spiritually so that the fullness of Christ might be seen in your life in order that the appearing of the Lord will fulfill Romans 8:19.

Conclusion

If this book has opened your eyes, may I ask if you have received Salvation which is the Passover feast? Do you know the Lord as your Savior? If not, speak openly with Him and repent of your sins. If you have done so, have you received the gifts of the Spirit of 1 Corinthians 12, which is the feast of Pentecost? If not, ask of Him for He will give it to you. If you have experienced the first two feasts, might I suggest that you come to the Lord in the Feast of Tabernacles? The third experience will lift you up above all battles and into total union with Him.

Bibliography

Cassirer, Heinz W. God's New Covenant, A New Testament Translation. Grand Rapids: William B. Eerdmans Publishing Co., 1989.

Companion Bible. Grand Rapids: Kregel Publications, 1990.

Eby, J. Preston. "The Coming of the Lord." Kingdom Bible Studies. El Paso, Texas.

Graham, Billy. Angels: God's Secret Agents. Garden City, NY: Doubleday and Co.

Hislop, Alexander. The Two Babylons. Neptune, New Jersey: Loizeaux Brothers, 1916.

Jukes, Andrew. Four Views of Christ. Grand Rapids: Kregel Publications, 1901.

Lubbers, George. The Bible versus Millenial Teaching. Grand Rapids: by author 2274 Cranbrook Dr. N.E., 1989.

Martin, Walter. The Kingdom of the Cults. Minneapolis: Bethany Fellowship Inc., 1965.

McConnell, William. The Gift of Time. Downers Grove, IL: Inter-Varsity Press, 1983.

Milton, Terry. Biblical Apocalyptics. Grand Rapids: Baker, 1988.

Moffatt, James The Bible, A New Translation. New York: Harper & Row, 1954

Nisbett, N. The Prophecy of the Destruction of Jerusalem. London: Simmons and Kirby Co., 1787.

Reilly, James. Union: A Treatise on the Consanguity and Affinity Between Christ and the Church. Philadelphia: Gihon, Fairchild & Co., 1843.

Rotherham, Joseph. The Emphasized Bible. Grand Rapids: Kregel Publications, 1971.

Russell, J. Stuart, The Parousia. Grand Rapids: Baker, 1887.

Weston, Charles Gilbert. The Weston Study Bible. Jefferson, OR: Weston Bible Ministries, 1993.

Willhite, Lloyd and Jim Bias. "Time Line." Porter, OK.

Young, Robert. Young's Literal Translation of the Holy Bible. Grand Rapids: Baker, 1898.

Zodhiates, Spiros. The Hebrew-Greek Key Study Bible. Chattanooga, TN.: AMG Publishers, 1991.